# 40 Days to
## Starting Over

*Juanita Bynum*

# 40 Days to
## Starting Over

*No More Sheets Challenge*

DESTINY IMAGE® PUBLISHERS, INC.

P.O. Box 310, Shippensburg, PA 17257-0310

*"Speaking to the Purposes of God for This Generation and for the Generations to Come."*

This book and all other Destiny Image, Revival Press, MercyPlace, Fresh Bread, Destiny Image Fiction, and Treasure House books are available at Christian bookstores and distributors worldwide.

For a U.S. bookstore nearest you, call 1-800-722-6774.

For more information on foreign distributors, call 717-532-3040.

Reach us on the Internet: www.destinyimage.com.

ISBN 13 TP: 978-0-7684-3279-4

ISBN 13 Ebook: 978-0-7684-9054-1

For Worldwide Distribution, Printed in the U.S.A.

2 3 4 5 6 7 8 9 10 11 / 18 17 16 15

# Contents

# Introduction

Let me say to you essentially what I said to readers of *No More Sheets*: You did not purchase this journal for mere information or entertainment. You are entering a 40-day journey to relocate your body parts. You are reading and journaling to find your identity.[1] You are reading these words at this moment in time because you want victory over the sheets.

My prayer is that, by the time you complete Day 40, you will have met the person you lost so long ago. You will have become reacquainted with who you really are and *you are going to like who you see.*[2]

Those are outstanding outcomes and well worth achieving! I encourage you—with every fiber of my being—to dig in and interact with each page. Enter the daily entries prayerfully and with a heart that is open to God. Consider what you are reading; confront yourself with the truths you discover. Then engage each question thoughtfully. Answer it honestly and without the weight of shame or condemnation. God sees your heart. He knows why you are here. He will work with you and in you to produce the change that you and He desire.

As you write out your answers, you will learn more than you can imagine—about God, about yourself, and about your future. That's the beauty of journaling. It is a healing process between you and God. It brings you face to face with self-diminishing thoughts, misconceptions, and misunderstandings that operate in the background of your life. It will help you to pinpoint these deceivers and root them out of your heart.

Completing this journal will also help you to remember what you really want and who you are destined by God to be. It will remind you that who and what you are has absolutely nothing to do with what you do; it has everything to do with what Christ has done. He paid the price—*in full.*

You are His beloved. He has not left you to your own devices. He stands ready to lead you—day by day…inch by inch…moment by moment. I know, because He has done it for me through many ups and downs, many good times and many days of sorrow.

My prayer for you is an all-out prayer of victory in Christ. The apostle Paul stated it perfectly and now I pray this for you:

> *That the God of our Lord Jesus Christ, the Father of glory, may give unto you the spirit of wisdom and revelation in the knowledge of Him: the eyes of your understanding being enlightened; that ye may know what is the hope of His calling, and what the riches of the glory of His inheritance in the saints, and what is the exceeding greatness of His power to us-ward who believe, according to the working of His mighty power, which He wrought in Christ, when He raised Him from the dead, and set Him at His own right hand in the heavenly places, far above all principality, and power, and might, and dominion, and every name that is named, not only in this world, but also in that which is to come: and hath put all things under His feet, and gave Him to be the head over all things to the church, which is His body, the fulness of Him that filleth all in all* (Ephesians 1:17-23).

Your freedom march begins now. *No more sheets!*

## ENDNOTES

1. Juanita Bynum, *No More Sheets: Starting Over,* revised edition (Shippensburg, PA: Destiny Image Publishers, 2010), 25.

2. Ibid.

# About Those Sheets

*And when He [Jesus] thus had spoken, He cried with a loud voice, Lazarus, come forth. And he that was dead came forth, bound hand and foot with graveclothes: and his face was bound about with a napkin. Jesus saith unto them, Loose him, and let him go* (John 11:43-44).

# Today's Devotion

...Sheets are layers of bondage that have affected your emotions through sexual experiences. A lot of single men and women are bound up today. Sisters are carrying the baggage of past relationships and sexual encounters. Brothers aren't free to answer God's call on their lives. Weighed down with guilt, shame, and regret, these believers have become ineffective for the Kingdom....You see, sheets will affect your walk with God.

Don't think you're exempt because you're a Christian. If you jumped in and out of the sheets with someone who was not your spouse, those sexual experiences have bound you up. It will take work to get free, and you are going to need some help!...

Yes, you may be born again. You may have experienced resurrection power. But you may be unable to enjoy the blessings of God because of those sheets. Like Lazarus, you need those grave clothes to loose you and let you go.

(*No More Sheets*, Revised Edition, Pages 33-34)

# CHALLENGE THE SHEETS

1. Often, the sheets have their way with us because we are blinded to the bondage they bring. Has this blindness operated in your life? Explain. When were your eyes opened, and how?

_____

_____

_____

_____

_____

_____

_____

_____

_____

2. How has the weight of guilt, shame, or regret affected your overall demeanor? How might you feel freer to serve in the Kingdom without the sheets?

_____

_____

_____

_____

_____

_____

_____

_____

3. Breaking out of the sheets requires some effort. Like any process, it begins
   with a first step. What first step will you take today?

_____

_____

_____

_____

_____

_____

4. How has being in the sheets hindered you from enjoying God's blessings? Be
   specific.

_____

_____

_____

_____

_____

_____

5. What kind of help do you need to be loosed from the "grave clothes" that
   are the sheets? Who might be able to provide that help?

_____

_____

_____

_____

_____

_____

# MEDITATION

Over the years, God has shown me how to rid myself of layers of sheets that had affected my work for Him. It was a painful process. I learned the hard way, but you don't have to.... I know the emotional devastation they can cause. Gradually, however, you become comfortable with them. You may have been wrapped in them so long that you can't imagine life any other way. But if you want to enjoy the fullness of God, you must cast off those sheets. You must make this declaration for every future relationship: No more sheets!

(*No More Sheets*, Revised Edition, Page 34)

> How would you describe the emotional devastation of being in the sheets? How does the "comfort" of the sheets prove to be false comfort in the long run?

_____

_____

_____

_____

_____

_____

_____

_____

_____

_____

_____

_____

_____

_____

_____

# DAY 2

# One Flesh

*Therefore shall a man leave his father and his mother, and shall cleave unto his wife: and they shall be one flesh* (Genesis 2:24).

# Today's Devotion

The whole concept of *No More Sheets* is based on a husband and a wife knowing each other and becoming "one flesh".... Today we go through a marriage ceremony just for the sake of saying, "I'm married." The spoken vow is not as important as it once was. In Bible days, your word was your bond. If a father gave his daughter to a man who vowed to take her as his wife, and the man had intercourse with the daughter, that marriage was consummated....

The Lord told me that there will be no more sheets. There will be no more acts in which men lay down with women and shed blood on the sheets without vowing to stay with them for life. This has to cease in the Body of Christ.

Deuteronomy 12:19 says that the power of intercourse was such that once a man had slept with the woman, he was not allowed to put her away...ever. That law still stands today. We cannot take intercourse lightly. It is an act of covenant, an act of marriage that joins two souls together. That's where we get the term *soul ties.*

(*No More Sheets,* Revised Edition, Pages 34-36)

# CHALLENGE THE SHEETS

1. The term *one flesh* has powerful implications that are often overlooked in today's world. How do these implications impact your view of the marriage vows?

_____

_____

_____

_____

_____

_____

2. What is the importance of a husband and wife becoming one flesh? What are some of the benefits you have witnessed in your life or the lives of others?

_____

_____

_____

_____

_____

_____

_____

3. Is your word your bond? How does your level of integrity guide you when sexual temptation beckons? How does your commitment to integrity affect your life overall?

_____

_____

_____

_____

_____

4. If you have been in the sheets, how did you feel afterward? With Genesis 2:24 in mind, explain why you felt that way. How would you feel differently after sex within the bans of marriage?

_____

_____

_____

_____

_____

5. Intercourse is a covenant act that ties two souls together. How do these soul ties affect your life when they are formed outside of marriage? Within marriage?

_____

_____

_____

_____

_____

_____

# MEDITATION

When a man enters your body, he comes to stay. You and he are one. We take that for granted. When a man has intercourse with you, he adds his life to yours. When he leaves, his body is no longer there, but his spirit is; you are left with only the weight of the memory. The woman is left devastated. It's as if someone walks out of your life, splits you in half, and then says, "Just go your own way." That's why there is such a cry from the realm of the spirit—no more sheets!

(*No More Sheets*, Revised Edition, Pages 36-37)

> Does reading the preceding paragraph help you to understand powerful emotions you have experienced in the past? Will you love yourself enough to say, "No more sheets; I won't allow myself to be split in half again"? Where will your answer—whether *yes* or *no*—lead you?

_____

_____

_____

_____

_____

_____

_____

_____

_____

_____

_____

_____

_____

# Spirit Versus Flesh

*For the flesh lusteth against the Spirit, and the Spirit against the flesh: and these are contrary the one to the other: so that ye cannot do the things that ye would* (Galatians 5:17).

# Today's Devotion

We must understand that the Bible says that we are not debtors to the flesh. We don't owe the flesh anything. The flesh can't compensate your spirit. The flesh and the spirit are not in cooperation, but they are in competition....

For too long we've depended on the flesh to do what only the Spirit can do. People have tried to deliver you from your flesh while working in the flesh. If I would allow it, my flesh would supersede my spirit, making me hold back on what I need to say. The Scripture says that my flesh desires to do anything that my spirit does not want to do. The apostle Paul wrote that these two are contrary to one another. That means if my flesh says yes, my spirit says no....

God told me that His people have heard enough junk. They have heard enough Bible stories that tickle their ears, but still allow them to live comfortably while doing fleshly things. I sense very strongly that the Lord is fed up with people being comfortable in their lustful ways while no one addresses the issues.

(*No More Sheets*, Revised Edition, Pages 42-43)

# CHALLENGE THE SHEETS

1. How has the competition between your flesh and spirit been witnessed through specific situations in your life? In the midst of the struggle, do you feel empowered to make sound spiritual choices, or do you feel as though your flesh has ultimate control? Are your feelings accurate or misleading? How so?

_____

_____

_____

_____

_____

_____

_____

_____

2. How do your views of the struggle between the flesh and the spirit affect your life outcomes? Be specific.

_____

_____

_____

_____

_____

_____

_____

3. Have you ever tried to overcome the sheets by depending solely upon your own strength? How does this differ from depending upon the Spirit?

_____

_____

_____

_____

_____

_____

4. To what degree are you comfortable entertaining fleshly pursuits, whether in thought or deed? What does your comfort level reveal?

_____

_____

_____

_____

_____

_____

5. How do you respond when a trusted friend or loved one addresses a sensitive issue in your life? What emotions and beliefs are at work in your response?

_____

_____

_____

_____

_____

_____

_____

# MEDITATION

The only person who can adequately address these issues is someone who has experienced them. When God places a mandate on your life, He will lead you to do risky things—things that make you feel uncomfortable and vulnerable—so understand that if He doesn't walk you through the process, you will miserably fail. Without the Lord to govern the things I do and say, I am a hopeless case. I am totally dependent on His Lordship in my life.

(*No More Sheets*, Revised Edition, Page 43)

> When you rely on the Holy Spirit rather than your flesh, you can handle the risks He asks you to take. Are you ready to admit that without Him, you, too, are a "hopeless case"? What specific decisions will you make to reflect this realization?

# The Right Kind of Nakedness

*And Noah began to be an husbandman, and he planted a vine-yard: and he drank of the wine, and was drunken; and he was uncovered within his tent. And Ham, the father of Canaan, saw the nakedness of his father, and told his two brethren without* (Genesis 9:20-22).

## Today's Devotion

Christians often forget that we are not on a playground, but a battleground. The Lord told us to prepare for warfare. Entrenched in the very idea of war is an understanding that there will be some wounds. This is a very important lesson: We must learn to survive the wounds....

Even as I write, I must fight the groans of my flesh that tell me to pull down the shades. Why? My hesitancy reveals an important issue in the Body: We are so afraid of someone taking advantage of our nakedness that we keep ourselves totally covered.... In order to be free, we must remove the masks....

I understand that people may violate you at your most vulnerable moment. Sometimes even those closest to you will take advantage of you. They appear to be coming to your rescue while contemplating your demise. In order for me to really open up, I must risk the possibility of even my closest friends or family members taking my secrets and trying to use them against me.

But do you know what I love about God? He gives us examples of what we're going through to let us know that someone else has gone through it, too.

(*No More Sheets*, Revised Edition, Pages 45-46)

# CHALLENGE THE SHEETS

1. As Noah learned, being naked is risky; yet, the right kind of nakedness is necessary for growth. How can you expose your wounds to the "air" in a way that balances wisdom and godly vulnerability? Whom can you take into your confidence?

_____

_____

_____

_____

_____

_____

_____

_____

_____

2. What mask(s) have you worn to protect yourself? How do they encumber your daily life? What might freedom from these masks look like?

_____

_____

_____

_____

_____

_____

_____

_____

3. Can you remember a time when someone close to you took advantage of your "nakedness"? How does this experience relate to the mask(s) you described in answer to Question 2?

_____

_____

_____

_____

_____

_____

4. In the context of life as a spiritual battleground, are you more or less willing to risk being wounded now than you were in the past? What has changed?

_____

_____

_____

_____

_____

5. How might God use your risk-taking for His purposes in the lives of others? How would this process ultimately affect your life?

_____

_____

_____

_____

_____

_____

# MEDITATION

...If I offend you, bear with me. If I insult you, tolerate me. If I embarrass you, understand me. But I have to take you through the process of purification. I must use the anointing on my life to liberate you at all cost.

I have a mandate from Heaven to solidify singles so they may find satisfaction in a Savior. I must divulge some truths to the divorced so they can reach their divine destination. I also must challenge the couples so they can be more than conquerors in Christ. Finally, I must offer hope to a dying world so that they can have all that God has promised them.

(*No More Sheets,* Revised Edition, Page 47)

> We are wading into the deep waters where prickly issues are confronted. Have you felt offended, insulted, or embarrassed as you read and respond to this journal? How might those momentary wounds bring freedom in the long run?

_____

_____

_____

_____

_____

_____

_____

_____

_____

_____

_____

# DAY 5

# Walk in My Moccasins

*Seeing then that we have a great high priest, that is passed into the heavens, Jesus the Son of God, let us hold fast our profession. For we have not an high priest which cannot be touched with the feeling of our infirmities; but was in all points tempted like as we are, yet without sin* (Hebrews 4:14-15).

# Today's Devotion

If a person has never seen a strawberry, she can't tell me what a strawberry looks, feels, or tastes like. The person could not describe the coarse outer texture that sends a certain sensation to the tongue. She can't tell me that the meat inside is smooth and gives an interesting contrast to the coarse outer layers. Being able to describe a strawberry indicates that a person has actually experienced this fruit....

I have heard many messages on how to cope with, confront, or conquer being single. Many of these talks would have carried greater weight if the speaker wasn't going home to his spouse while I returned to the lonely confines of my home.

Wouldn't you like to hear "Hold on!" from someone who's holding on themselves? If that married speaker rolls over in the sheets with their mate, they don't understand the ache in my heart. If they indulge in back-rubs from their mate, they can't fathom my longing to be touched.

(*No More Sheets,* Revised Edition, Pages 49-50)

# CHALLENGE THE SHEETS

1. Sometimes, you need to hear from someone who has "been there and done that." Is there someone whose experience is similar to yours and whom you can trust with your confidence? How might sharing your struggles with them help you to stand strong?

_____

_____

_____

_____

_____

_____

_____

_____

2. Can you recall a message that spoke directly to your situation and touched your heart? Is it still at work in your life, or have you lost sight of it? What is one point from that message that you need to be reminded of today?

_____

_____

_____

_____

_____

_____

_____

3. When someone who does not share your life experience speaks truth into your life, are you willing to hear them out? If they bring correction, are you open to receiving it, even knowing they haven't experienced the exact pain you have suffered?

_____

_____

_____

_____

_____

4. Are you surprised to learn that well-known ministers face the same struggles you do? How does knowing this help you?

_____

_____

_____

_____

_____

_____

5. Describe the ache in your heart that you wish others could understand. Have you shared that ache with your great High Priest, Jesus Christ? Why not share it with Him now?

_____

_____

_____

_____

_____

_____

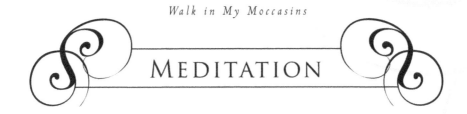

# MEDITATION

I know what it's like to taste bitter tears in the middle of the night, just wishing someone was there to hold me. I know what it's like to believe God for a prayer that seems like it will never be answered. I know what it feels like to wonder if my time will ever come. Only a person who has experienced my pain can tell me that they know how I feel.

(*No More Sheets*, Revised Edition, Page 50)

> Have you cried bitter tears in the middle of the night, wondering if your prayer will ever be answered? What prayer is on your lips right now? Are you willing to wait for God's answer?

_____

_____

_____

_____

_____

_____

_____

_____

_____

_____

_____

_____

_____

_____

_____

DAY 6

# It's True Anyhow

*Confess your faults one to another, and pray one for another, that ye may be healed. The effectual fervent prayer of a righteous man availeth much* (James 5:16).

## Today's Devotion

I have been in services where a preacher told me to write a former boyfriend's name on a piece of paper, crumble the paper, and then throw it over my shoulder while telling the devil that it's over. After all that, the same problem was still sticking to me like my skin.…

Some of you want me to give you a bunch of hallelujahs and praise the Lords and tell you that I'm just running for Jesus and haven't gotten tired yet. I am not going to perpetrate a lie. I get tired many times, but His Word strengthens me every day! That's right. The process is one day at a time. I wrestle every day of my life to walk in the integrity of the Word.

Yes, I am Prophetess Juanita Bynum, but I am not dead. I know you think that you cannot be anointed and still have a desire to sleep with someone. Some think that because I am anointed, I never get frustrated. They think that I never want to have some serious sex. They think that I don't ever want to do something wrong. Let me tell you that the devil is a liar. If you're telling that lie, then you're a liar, too.

(*No More Sheets*, Revised Edition, Pages 51-52)

# CHALLENGE THE SHEETS

1. How is it that we can claim a wrong relationship to be over, only to discover that it is still stuck to us like a second skin?

_____

_____

_____

_____

_____

_____

_____

_____

2. Everyone is in a battle and everyone gets tired. Why is it so important to understand this truth? Why is it important to admit that it's true for us?

_____

_____

_____

_____

_____

_____

_____

_____

3. How do you lean into the Word when you are weary? How does it help you to maintain your integrity?

_____

_____

_____

_____

_____

4. I am very frank about the reality of sexual temptation in my life. Does that shock you? If so, why? How can it also help to set you free from condemnation?

_____

_____

_____

_____

_____

_____

5. The devil wants each of us to believe that we are the only ones who struggle with sexual desires. How does lying about ourselves empower him to keep us bound?

_____

_____

_____

_____

_____

_____

# MEDITATION

Every single day of my life, I struggle to crucify my flesh. If you told the truth, you would say the same thing. I know what it feels like to go to the mall or the laundromat and see fine men everywhere I turn. Sometimes I wish I wasn't a prophetess. I think, "I wish I could give this man my cell number or my office phone number. No one has to know. I will do this just one time. I can get away with it." But we know that's not true.

(*No More Sheets*, Revised Edition, Page 52)

> Read Galatians 5:24-25. What does it mean to crucify your flesh? Who stands ready to help you do it?

# Temptation: Only a Test

*Wherefore let him that thinketh he standeth take heed lest he fall. There hath no temptation taken you but such as is common to man: but God is faithful, who will not suffer you to be tempted above that ye are able; but will with the temptation also make a way to escape, that ye may be able to bear it* (I Corinthians 10:12-13).

# Today's Devotion

Let's make one thing clear: Temptations are not wrong. Yielding to a temptation is wrong. Many Christians have been deceived by the devil into thinking that just because they want to do it, they may as well go ahead and do it. If we did not want to do it, it would not be a temptation.

Temptation is designed to test your resistance. It doesn't mean that you automatically fail just because you were given the test. The teacher must grade your answers before he determines whether you pass or fail.

Many of us think that when the enemy hands us the test, we have failed. That is not true. Your grade is determined by how you answer the questions on the test. This is what's wrong with many of us in ministry—we see our name on the test and become bewildered. We didn't think we should have been given a test at all; consequently, we don't tell the world that we had a test. We want everyone to believe we are exempt, but that's a lie.

(*No More Sheets*, Revised Edition, Page 55)

# CHALLENGE THE SHEETS

1. What is the difference between being tempted and yielding to temptation? Give examples of each from personal experience.

_____

_____

_____

_____

_____

_____

_____

_____

2. Clearly, the devil wants you to believe that when temptation crosses your mind, you are in sin. Explain how this deception may have contributed to your yielding to temptation in the past.

_____

_____

_____

_____

_____

_____

_____

_____

3. If you are like me, you have been tempted thousands of times. Does knowing the truth about temptation remove an unnecessary weight from your shoulders? Explain.

_____

_____

_____

_____

_____

_____

_____

4. How can you be strengthened and even empowered by the testing of your resistance? How can the enemy's influence be weakened by it?

_____

_____

_____

_____

_____

_____

_____

5. How has temptation resulted in misplaced shame in your life? How has this shame enticed you to pretend that you are exempt from temptation?

_____

_____

_____

_____

_____

_____

_____

# MEDITATION

Don't even pretend like you're Peter Pan or Tinkerbell in the Body of Christ—so strong in every area and flying so high in the Spirit that your feet never touch the ground.... Just because you are standing today, that doesn't mean that you might not fall tomorrow.... The very second you drop your guard, you may as well expect a hit. That very thought implies that we are vulnerable.... Sheets don't discriminate. They will try to wrap up any body.

(*No More Sheets*, Revised Edition, Pages 53-55)

> Are you wearing a mask of invulnerability? What kind of pressure is that adding to your life? Consider your reasons for wearing the mask and ask yourself, "Is it worth it?"

_____

_____

_____

_____

_____

_____

_____

_____

_____

_____

_____

_____

_____

_____

# Seducing Spirits and Self-esteem

*God said, Let us make man in our image, after our likeness: and let them have dominion over the fish of the sea, and over the fowl of the air, and over the cattle, and over all the earth, and over every creeping thing that creepeth upon the earth. So God created man in His own image, in the image of God created He him; male and female created He them* (Genesis 1:26-27).

# Today's Devotion

Have you ever met somebody and decided in your heart that this is it?... That's what happened to me in 1978. I met a guy who...I felt could really make me happy. But, he could not decide between another girl and me. My self-esteem was so low that I was willing to accept mere crumbs from the relationship.... When you allow a situation like this, a man will give you just enough to keep you hooked, but not enough to say, "I do."

A mutual friend called one night to say, "Juanita, you're a beautiful woman, and you don't have to settle for this. He's not as committed to you as you think he is."

"I don't believe that," I told her.

"Hold on the phone line while I call him. Don't say anything—just listen."

What did I hear?

...He told my friend. "She's a very beautiful woman, but I'm leaning toward this other woman...."

When I heard that, it devastated me. I lived with the expectation that perhaps he would leave this other girl and come to me. When it didn't happen, I felt very rejected. I buried that hurt and started looking for love in all the wrong places.

(*No More Sheets*, Revised Edition, Pages 61-63)

# CHALLENGE THE SHEETS

1. Have you ever misjudged a relationship and over-invested in someone who didn't feel the same way about you? Explain.

_____

_____

_____

_____

_____

_____

_____

_____

_____

2. Did self-esteem play a role in the dynamics of your relationship? How did your self-image skew your vision?

_____

_____

_____

_____

_____

_____

_____

_____

3. How was your well-being compromised to keep the relationship alive? How was your value as a human being diminished?

_____

_____

_____

_____

_____

4. When self-esteem is low, we tend to make others "bigger" and "more important" than us. What message does that convey to others and what kind of treatment does it invite?

_____

_____

_____

_____

_____

_____

5. Rejection can be devastating when self-esteem is low. Do you have any buried hurts waiting to be healed? Why not lift them up to God in prayer? He desires to heal you!

_____

_____

_____

_____

_____

# MEDITATION

Seducing spirits usually attach themselves to people who, for some reason or another, suffer from low self-esteem.... When searching for love in all the wrong places, you'll find only masks hiding deceitful faces.... You're not a cheap thrill. Your purpose must be fulfilled; therefore, stay still until you know God's perfect will.

(*No More Sheets*, Revised Edition, Pages 62-63)

> Have you placed someone on a pedestal and opened the door to seducing spirits in the process? When you consider the One in whose image you were created, how does your self-image change?

# DAY 9

# Confusing "Chemistry"

*Marriage is honourable in all, and the bed undefiled: but whore-mongers and adulterers God will judge* (Hebrews 13:4).

## Today's Devotion

We're to replace worldly ideologies, concepts, and philosophies with the principles of the Kingdom and Word of God. Approaching sex outside of God creates its own blanket of residue on you. Do you know what the results are? You'll find yourself attracted to people who are not purged, just like you. These people are not the mates God intended for you.

We say that we just "clicked." We have "chemistry." No, what you have is the same perverted spirit. You have the same unclean nature, and spirits attract their own kind. This is how you end up with someone who you think is for you. However, when you go through the process of purification, you will see that he's far from the right person. The difference will blow your mind.

That's why people who are considering marriage must seek godly counsel. Many people say that they will make it because they just love each other. You may think you're in love, but you just may be after sex, and sex doesn't need true love to operate. Sex will take care of itself.

(*No More Sheets*, Revised Edition, Page 66)

# CHALLENGE THE SHEETS

1. To what degree have you applied the principles of the Kingdom and Word of God to your love life? Have you cherry-picked certain principles and ignored others? What results have you experienced?

_____

_____

_____

_____

_____

_____

_____

2. Just as your physical appearance and dress attract certain kinds of people, the residue of ungodly sex becomes a "garment" that attracts those who are not purged. Has this kind of pattern emerged in your life? Explain.

_____

_____

_____

_____

_____

_____

_____

_____

_____

3. When you sense a special "chemistry" with someone, are you more likely to accept his or her sexual advances? How can you test the spiritual undercurrents and protect yourself from being vulnerable in this way?

4. Are you becoming aware of a relationship that was or is based on a perverted form of chemistry? How has your new understanding altered your perception of the relationship? What does this mean for the future?

5. Where does sex fit into your working definition of *love?* To what degree has genuine love driven your relationship decisions? How might your working definition of *love* need to be fine-tuned?

# MEDITATION

Sex is not all there is to marriage. When touching, handling, and fondling enter your relationship, it distorts your focus on the spirit of the person. Instead, your attention is drawn to their flesh. You begin to desire each other's genitals more than you begin to desire to see the Spirit of God in each other. You can always tell when it's that kind of relationship because when there is no sex, you don't have anything to talk about.

(*No More Sheets*, Revised Edition, Pages 66-67)

> If you are currently involved in a relationship, are you focused on the spirit of the person and on whom he or she is becoming? How do your choices reveal your focus?

_____

_____

_____

_____

_____

_____

_____

_____

_____

_____

_____

_____

_____

_____

# Choose God's Way

*Be careful for nothing; but in every thing by prayer and supplication with thanksgiving let your requests be made known unto God* (Philippians 4:6).

## Today's Devotion

When I married in 1981…I was clueless. I didn't consider ministering to my man. I didn't think about what he had been through. I didn't concern myself with staying on my knees to press him to another level in God. I was too young and immature to understand the power of carrying the weight of someone else's life. When everyone told me that our problems weren't my fault, I accepted that as the truth.

It wasn't so much as the wrong done to me—he was just being himself. You have to research his background enough to realize what you're getting. But remember this: you promised to love and cherish. You vowed to protect and minister to him. It was a lie. Don't blame anyone else. You just lied. Many of us don't want to admit it, but that's what really happened. We did not know the real weight of those words.

This starts us down the road to the sheets. We feel comfortable when we can blame the other person. Deep down, we know that it's really our fault, too.

(*No More Sheets*, Revised Edition, Page 68)

# CHALLENGE THE SHEETS

I. Often, we marry having all the benefits of marriage in mind, but without praying first and counting the cost. Whether you are currently married, divorced, or single, are there spiritual responsibilities in marriage that you have not considered until now? What are they?

_____

_____

_____

_____

_____

_____

_____

_____

_____

_____

2. How are marital responsibilities connected to the truth that husband and wife are one flesh?

_____

_____

_____

_____

_____

_____

_____

3. Is it possible for relational challenges to be entirely the fault of one person? Explain your response.

_____

_____

_____

_____

_____

4. If you are married or in a serious relationship, did you research the background of your significant other before making a serious commitment? How does avoidance of this step affect the foundation of your commitment?

_____

_____

_____

_____

_____

5. If you are married, did you realize the weight of your promise to love and cherish? How has this realization (or lack thereof) played out in your marriage? If you are single, how can you get a firm grasp on the weight of possible future vows?

_____

_____

_____

_____

_____

_____

# MEDITATION

Do you know that the proper method to receive anything from God is by prayer and supplication?... If your mate has not come through prayer and supplication, then you have chosen that mate illegally. Your relationship has a shaky foundation. Only deep repentance by both parties can repair the damage. If you date and marry in the flesh, I can tell you this: expect extra, extra, extra problems along with the problems that marriage already comes with.

That's exactly what happened to me. My husband and I had additional conflicts in our marriage that we couldn't resolve. I had no idea that the next several years would take me through hell on earth.

(*No More Sheets*, Revised Edition, Pages 68-69)

> Where does prayer figure into a current or past relationship? If prayerlessness contributed to a shaky foundation, are you praying now? How can prayer and repentance change your situation for the better?

_____

_____

_____

_____

_____

_____

_____

_____

_____

_____

# Credit Where Credit Is Due

*But He knoweth the way that I take: when He hath tried me, I shall come forth as gold.... For he performeth the thing that is appointed for me: and many such things are with him* (Job 23:10,14).

# Today's Devotion

Some of you might be saying, "You've certainly been through a lot! What about your husband? What did he do to you? What kind of man was he to cause you such pain?"

God has given me a platform to speak to the Body of Christ. It's very easy to forget about those people who don't have a platform. It is easy to take that power and misuse it by telling my whole story. Exploiting my ex-husband does not make me a better person. Talking about him doesn't make me more than I really am. That is not necessary.

I could say, "Well, he did this and he did that. Oh, honey, let me tell you some things about him." But that's not what caused my relationship or my mind to go bad. What I *allowed* in my life put me in those situations.

I was already messed up when I got married. I already had low self-esteem, and I already had issues with my character that were not resolved. There was no discipline in my life.

(*No More Sheets*, Revised Edition, Page 83)

# CHALLENGE THE SHEETS

1. Every relationship, whether good or bad, takes two. Would broadcasting the shortcomings of your ex help you to feel better about yourself or worse? Explain.

_____

_____

_____

_____

_____

_____

_____

_____

_____

2. How does shouting your ex's faults from the mountaintops affect your personal growth and healing?

_____

_____

_____

_____

_____

_____

_____

_____

_____

3. List the setbacks and disappointments you have suffered due to a current or past relationship. What positives can you take from them? What negatives should you let go?

_____

_____

_____

_____

_____

_____

4. How did your choices expose you to negative outcomes? How would you do things differently today?

_____

_____

_____

_____

_____

_____

5. Are there any unresolved character issues that predispose you to relational failures? What are they and how can you address them?

_____

_____

_____

_____

_____

_____

# MEDITATION

By the grace of God, I yielded to His discipline. That's when He began to refine me.... I could have said, "I can't stand men because of all that I've been through. I hate my husband. Because of him, I had to endure welfare, anorexia nervosa, and a nervous breakdown." But you don't get healed that way. I had to admit that those things happened because...I didn't have wisdom to avoid those snares. I heard a preacher say that bitterness has a porcupine effect on your inner man. When you harbor bitterness, it gets in your belly and tears you up. You don't destroy anyone but yourself.

(*No More Sheets*, Revised Edition, Page 84)

> What choices can you make to ensure that, like Job, you will come forth
> as gold? Which porcupine quills can you pluck out? Where can you
> yield to God's discipline more fully?

_____

_____

_____

_____

_____

_____

_____

_____

_____

_____

_____

_____

_____

# Look in the Mirror

*If any be a hearer of the word, and not a doer, he is like unto a man beholding his natural face in a glass: for he beholdeth himself, and goeth his way, and straightway forgetteth what manner of man he was* (James 1:23-24).

# Today's Devotion

You need to explore what it is about you that may not be right; do this before you dwell on what was not right in your mate. You can't change your mate, you can only change you. That's why I had to forgive my ex-husband....

When you make marriage vows and don't fulfill them, a lot happens. You disappoint God, your spouse, and yourself. You get caught in a negative cycle of blame, guilt, and regret. This leads to self-pity. This spirit says, "I'm nothing. I'm worthless. I'll never be anything." Eventually, the spirit of your mind will regulate you to a level where you don't belong. While you are debased, lowlife people become attracted to you.

That's the beginning mindset of your sheets. Why? Because you feel you have to go to bed with someone to prove your womanhood or manhood, and sometimes that means anybody; therein lays the problem....

Sexuality in marriage is God's way of adding life to your life. When you marry for the wrong reason, life is added to death, which produces nothing but death and destruction in your spirit and emotions. Nothing will work out.

(*No More Sheets*, Revised Edition, Pages 84-85)

# CHALLENGE THE SHEETS

1. Often, we try to change others in order to avoid the fact that we are broken, too. How can an honest look in the mirror make us freer?

_____

_____

_____

_____

_____

_____

_____

_____

_____

2. Explain how blame, guilt, and regret lead to self-pity. How is self-pity self-limiting?

_____

_____

_____

_____

_____

_____

_____

_____

_____

3. How do our failures, perceived or otherwise, lead to self-abasement? How does knowing who we are in Christ keep us from regulating ourselves downward?

_____

_____

_____

_____

_____

_____

4. How does resting in this knowledge relieve us from having to prove ourselves in the sheets?

_____

_____

_____

_____

_____

_____

5. Sexuality in marriage is God's way of adding life to your life. How is sexuality in a future marriage affected by resorting to the sheets today?

_____

_____

_____

_____

_____

_____

# MEDITATION

Sex may be wonderful, but the enemy uses that to give you an illusion that your marriage is great when really it is not. One day you'll wake up and look in the mirror. Your eyes, which are the windows of your soul, can't hide the truth. You'll say to yourself, "I'm a dead woman. I'm a dead man. I've had good sex, but my spirit is dead."

If you are planning to get married soon, please ask yourself some questions. What is your level of process? Where are you in your level of purification? What damage are you about to do? Whose soul are you about to kill?

(*No More Sheets*, Revised Edition, Pages 85-86)

> Do you see how distorting God's intentions for sex can produce devastating results? How has your perspective of sex changed since beginning this 40-day journey?

# As Time Goes By

*Moreover the law entered, that the offence might abound. But where sin abounded, grace did much more abound: that as sin hath reigned unto death, even so might grace reign through righteousness unto eternal life by Jesus Christ our Lord* (Romans 5:20-21).

## Today's Devotion

Pit stops in the sheets are like putting a recorder on pause. You get out of the sheets and repent, someone hits play again. By the time you really get moving, you meet another man. Before you know it, you're back in the sheets. You hit the pause button a second time. After doing this for so many years, you've lost a lot of ground. Once you've finally realized what has happened, you're in your mid-thirties and way behind schedule. When you repent, God, in His mercy and purpose for your life, has to rush the process to put you back on schedule....

Isn't it good to know that when God has a plan for your life, He gets you to your destination? I don't care what kind of seeds the devil plants; when God has a plan for your life, He uses even your sheets to lead you to victory. He will turn every mistake into a ministry and then into a testimony.

(*No More Sheets*, Revised Edition, Pages 88-89)

# CHALLENGE THE SHEETS

1. Does it feel as though your life is a "recorder on pause"? Who controls the *pause* button? Who gets to hit *play* again?

_____

_____

_____

_____

_____

_____

_____

_____

_____

_____

2. How do the sheets disrupt your life? What is lost in the process? Is there any perceived gain? Explain.

_____

_____

_____

_____

_____

_____

_____

_____

_____

3. Do you feel that your life is "on schedule"? Describe how and why.

_____

_____

_____

_____

_____

_____

4. How does knowing that God has a plan for your life help to restore your hope and get you (or keep you) on track?

_____

_____

_____

_____

_____

_____

5. God can use our mistakes to lead us to victory. Describe how He has taken one of your mistakes and turned it into a testimony or ministry.

_____

_____

_____

_____

_____

_____

## MEDITATION

Someone might say that my ministry seems as if it has shot up overnight. Well, in some ways it did. God had to push me forth in a hurry because I was so late and behind schedule.... If you've made a mistake, it doesn't mean that life is over. God redeems even the worst situations. The apostle Paul, once a persecutor of the Church, understood... *"...where sin abounded, grace did much more abound..."* (Rom. 5:20). That grace is still available today, and it's available for you.

(*No More Sheets*, Revised Edition, Pages 88-89)

Have you ever felt as though your life was over? Do you feel that way now? What situation in your life do you want God to redeem and what role does His grace play in that process?

_____

_____

_____

_____

_____

_____

_____

_____

_____

_____

_____

_____

_____

_____

_____

# Take Time to Heal

*My times are in Thy hand: deliver me from the hand of mine enemies, and from them that persecute me. Make Thy face to shine upon Thy servant: save me for Thy mercies' sake* (Psalms 31:15-16).

# TODAY'S DEVOTION

About two weeks after my divorce, I got ready to go out. As I stood in front of the mirror, it dawned on me: "Oh my God, I'm single again." It was a strange feeling. Although it wasn't the best marriage, having a husband offered a sense of security. I felt I belonged with someone. Suddenly, I became fresh meat at the market.

I wasn't ready to date again. I needed a lot of emotional healing. I didn't understand it at the time, but now I know that when my husband left me, it was a sheet.

Let me explain. Remember, sheets are layers of emotional baggage that you get through sexual experiences. Even though we had a legal marriage, when he left me, it was a sheet. Something happens when you get a divorce. You don't trust yourself or your judgment anymore. The last time you said, "I do," you made a mistake. You ask yourself, "What if I make another mistake?"...

Have the courage to say, "Lord, until You are finished processing me, please don't send anyone my way."

(*No More Sheets*, Revised Edition, Pages 93-94)

# CHALLENGE THE SHEETS

1. Whether or not you have been through a divorce, you can probably relate to feeling alone after a breakup. Did you have a "moment in the mirror" when the realization hit you? Describe your emotions at the time.

_____

_____

_____

_____

_____

_____

_____

_____

2. Did the sense of being alone highlight memories of the relationship's positive features? What were they? Where did the positive features fit in a realistic assessment of the relationship?

_____

_____

_____

_____

_____

_____

_____

_____

_____

3. How would you describe the sense of belonging you experience(d) in a current or recent relationship? What does your description reveal about the relationship?

_____
_____
_____
_____
_____

4. Can you identify any baggage you picked up in past relationships? How has it shown up in a current or subsequent relationship?

_____
_____
_____
_____
_____

5. God always stands ready to relieve us of baggage and carry us through the healing process. Ask Him what the process is for your life; then be patient in allowing Him to take you through it.

_____
_____
_____
_____
_____

# MEDITATION

Being single again was a horrifying experience. I don't know how everyone else reacts to their divorce, but my eating spun out of control. Boy, was I a wreck. My figure ballooned from a size 9/10 to a size 16. During that period, my clothes became lethal weapons. My skirts were cutting off my circulation, and my turtlenecks from when I was skinny began to suffocate me. I began to be killed by my own wardrobe. I allowed my self-esteem to hit rock bottom, instead of allowing God to help me deal with the divorce. This was doubly bad. I became vulnerable to anyone who showed me any attention.

(*No More Sheets*, Revised Edition, Page 94)

> Have you experienced similar reactions to a divorce or breakup? Did your self-esteem plummet after the relationship ended? Or had low self-esteem operated during the relationship's better days?

0

# DAY 15

# Nourished by the Word

*Verily, verily, I say unto you, He that believeth on me hath everlasting life. I am that bread of life. Your fathers did eat manna in the wilderness, and are dead. This is the bread which cometh down from heaven, that a man may eat thereof, and not die* (John 6:47-50).

# Today's Devotion

While I was engaged to a guy, I visited a girlfriend one evening. She smiled and told me how proud she was of the way I was handling this guy's recent marriage. I glared at her and said, "What did you say?" She covered her mouth and asked, "Didn't you know?" Imagine my finding out that a guy I *thought* I was about to marry, had already married someone else. I fell off her barstool.

Do you want evidence that going to church is not enough? I didn't meditate on the Scripture I had just heard preached in church.... My reaction to what my girlfriend said simply shows that I was going to church, but not eating properly. A real "Yes, Lord!" was not in my soul. I was not agreeing with my pastor on that Word.

Do you know what I did? I bought the biggest bottle of whiskey I could find and got sloppy drunk. I was as drunk as five skunks.

Many of you have a hard time believing that. You ask, "Why would she do that?" That's a prime example of not having enough Word to sustain you during traumatic times.

(*No More Sheets*, Revised Edition, Pages 99-100)

# CHALLENGE THE SHEETS

1. Think of a time when you felt blindsided by bad news or a suddenly chang-ing situation. How spiritually prepared were you to discern and deal with the circumstances in a godly way? Explain.

_____

_____

_____

_____

_____

_____

_____

_____

2. What is your response to the Word? Does it find a place to settle in your heart? To what degree does it govern your decisions and actions?

_____

_____

_____

_____

_____

_____

_____

_____

_____

_____

3. Compare your focus on your spiritual nutrition with the level of your attention to your physical well-being. How would you characterize the balance between the two?

_____

_____

_____

_____

_____

4. When trauma strikes, what or whom do you reach for? Is your response guided by habit or by the Spirit of God?

_____

_____

_____

_____

_____

_____

5. The Word is sustenance provided for us by God Himself. How would you describe your appetite for the Word? Your intake? What do your answers reveal?

_____

_____

_____

_____

_____

_____

# MEDITATION

A carnal person always resorts to fleshly solutions. Alcohol was the only thing that made me feel better for that moment; it's like temporary relief. Some people drink. Some smoke. Others do drugs. I was a babe in the Lord and had not obtained a high Word level. I had no Word in me to defend or fight for me. Now when I say babe, I had been saved for over seven years; but years don't equal maturity. You see, years without quality feeding only means wasted years.... When you're not flowing in obedience, your flesh and a man can pull you away from God's will. You don't just step out; you take a quantum leap away from God.

(*No More Sheets*, Revised Edition, Pages 100-101)

> How often do you turn to God in worship, prayer, and the Word? How often do you turn to the world's ways of comforting the flesh or masking the pain?

_____

_____

_____

_____

_____

_____

_____

_____

_____

_____

_____

_____

# DAY 16

# Eviction Notice

*For the word of God is quick, and powerful, and sharper than any two-edged sword, piercing even to the dividing asunder of soul and spirit, and of the joints and marrow, and is a discerner of the thoughts and intents of the heart* (Hebrews 4:12).

# TODAY'S DEVOTION

I was trying to get out of the sheets, but the task was very difficult. Do you know why? I had fed on self-pity for so long that it had become a ruling or chief spirit in my life. A spirit that strong won't just pack his bags and go. You have to forcibly evict him. You simply take your spiritual weapon, which is the Word of God that is sharper than any two-edged sword, and use it to tear down imaginations and every high thing that exalts itself against the knowledge of God (see 2 Cor. 10:5)....

Only the Word of God is sharp enough to cut that thing away from your soul without destroying you as a person. I began to apply the Word and got better for a while, but that's the trick. It's like penicillin; you take it until the symptoms of the cold are gone, but if you don't finish the prescription, the virus is not completely killed. In the midst of my feeding break, I met someone else out of God's will. Yes, you guessed it: there I went again.... I was defeated by my own flesh.

(*No More Sheets*, Revised Edition, Pages 103-104)

# CHALLENGE THE SHEETS

1. Self-pity can keep you locked in the sheets. Pray, asking God to reveal the degree to which self-pity has become a ruling spirit in your life. Write down what He reveals.

---
---
---
---
---
---
---
---
---
---

2. Like any other demonic spirit, self-pity will stick around until he's forced to leave. How do you evict such a spirit?

---
---
---
---
---
---
---
---
---

3. Are any "imaginations" exalting themselves against the knowledge of God in your life? What are they?

_____

_____

_____

_____

_____

_____

_____

4. Explain the surgical manner in which the Word of God separates us from ungodliness.

_____

_____

_____

_____

_____

_____

_____

5. What happens when your "Word dosage" is interrupted? Even when healing in a particular area is complete, does your need for the Word lessen?

_____

_____

_____

_____

_____

_____

_____

# MEDITATION

When a spirit is cast out, he eventually tries to come back.... Picture this: The spirit is cast out. He and his buddies stand around wearing shades, smoking blunts, and drinking wine coolers, just waiting. They know that unless you fill that spot constantly with the Word of God, it's just a matter of time before they can send you another counterfeit and you will fall once again....

The enemy knows how you like your desserts. He knows what color you like. He knows which hairstyle appeals to you. He knows what kind of build will turn your head. Listen to me: the devil will definitely send you someone else.

(*No More Sheets*, Revised Edition, Page 105)

> Has the enemy ever set you up the way he did me? Is he setting you up right now? Are you strengthened in the Word and ready to brush off the counterfeits he sends your way?

_____

_____

_____

_____

_____

_____

_____

_____

_____

_____

_____

_____

_____

# Blinded by Sheets

*Now the Spirit speaketh expressly, that in the latter times some shall depart from the faith, giving heed to seducing spirits, and doctrines of devils; speaking lies in hypocrisy; having their conscience seared with a hot iron...* (I Timothy 4:1-2).

## TODAY'S DEVOTION

You can always tell when someone is in the sheets. These are some of the symptoms: that person will defy her parents, curse her sisters, throw her nose in the air, and defend herself to the last inch.

I know what I am talking about. You may say that you're not having sex. Even if no penetration has occurred, you've been aroused. That climax shuts down your ability to think clearly. Hormones are controlling you now—not your mind and definitely not your spirit. I know that's the truth. If you're honest, you know that's the truth, too.

We go into denial. The guy can be no good, but we say that he's so nice. We tell ourselves that no one understands him. No one else knows him like we do. We make excuses for him. We say something like, "His mother did him wrong and his father left him." Well, that's not your problem, but sheets make a person take on false burdens.

(*No More Sheets*, Revised Edition, Page 107)

# CHALLENGE THE SHEETS

1. Have you ever seen, in someone else's life, symptoms of being in the sheets? What were the symptoms? Have you ever had similar symptoms? Did you feel like others were watching?

_____

_____

_____

_____

_____

_____

_____

_____

2. Being in the sheets does not require penetration. Why isn't penetration the issue?

_____

_____

_____

_____

_____

_____

_____

_____

3. How does sexual arousal alter your decision-making and perceptions of your situation and behavior?

_____

_____

_____

_____

_____

_____

4. How does sexual involvement with someone other than your spouse increase your vulnerability to a wrong relationship? How does denial work in this scenario?

_____

_____

_____

_____

_____

_____

5. Sheets cause people to take on false burdens. Can you cite an example from your own life or from the life of someone you know?

_____

_____

_____

_____

_____

_____

# MEDITATION

Sheets make you think you are "Zena" or "Wonder Woman" or "The Bionic Woman." You ooze with compassion for him when you've never had that much mercy for your own family. You find grace that even God has never seen. Believe me, sheets will also help you justify why you must have your needs met.

Sheets blind you to the obvious. You won't care whether he has a job or not. You won't even ask him when he last held a job. Sheets manipulate you to go out with him and pay the bill yourself. You even find yourself doing things in public that are a dead giveaway that you are in the sheets.

(*No More Sheets*, Revised Edition, Page 108)

> Have the sheets ever blinded you to the truth? Did you lower your standards and settle for someone you knew was not right for you? What has it cost you?

_____

_____

_____

_____

_____

_____

_____

_____

_____

_____

_____

_____

_____

_____

# A Shepherd's Protection

*The Lord is my shepherd; I shall not want. He maketh me to lie down in green pastures: He leadeth me beside the still waters. He restoreth my soul: He leadeth me in the paths of righteousness for His name's sake. Yea, though I walk through the valley of the shadow of death, I will fear no evil: for Thou art with me; Thy rod and Thy staff they comfort me. Thou preparest a table before me in the presence of mine enemies: Thou anointest my head with oil; my cup runneth over. Surely goodness and mercy shall follow me all the days of my life: and I will dwell in the house of the Lord for ever* (Psalms 23:1-6).

## TODAY'S DEVOTION

Submitting to authority shields us from the enemy's deception. That's why God placed pastors in the Body of Christ....

Why doesn't your girlfriend or boyfriend want to meet your pastor? A shepherd has vision that we don't have. A shepherd stands taller than we stand. He can see farther down the road than we can see. If the person you are dating is afraid to meet your pastor, he or she is not God's will for your life. Even now, when someone asks me out to dinner, I tell him, "You have to meet my pastor first."

Pastor may look at me with raised eyebrows and that tells me, "Get rid of him. He's not the one." Listen: women know women and men know men. If you are afraid to take someone to meet your leader or pastor, then that person is not in God's will for your life. God placed leaders in our lives to watch over our souls. They are not against us. They are for us. That's why I would not advise anyone to date without seeking wise counsel about the person.

(*No More Sheets*, Revised Edition, Pages 115-116)

# CHALLENGE THE SHEETS

1.  Describe three qualities of a shepherd, as described in Psalm 23. Relate these qualities to the leader's role in regard to singles in the Church.

_____

_____

_____

_____

_____

_____

_____

_____

_____

_____

2.  If someone you are dating avoids meeting your pastor, what might the reason(s) be? How does this avoidance make you feel?

_____

_____

_____

_____

_____

_____

_____

_____

_____

_____

3. What do you think will happen if you tolerate this avoidance? What if you challenge it?

_____

_____

_____

_____

_____

_____

4. Have you ever avoided introducing your pastor to someone you dated? What motivated you? Did you rationalize your behavior? How?

_____

_____

_____

_____

_____

_____

5. Why is it important to expose the people you date to the people you trust? Explain why it is crucial to accept wise counsel about the people you date. What are the possible consequences of avoiding this step?

_____

_____

_____

_____

_____

_____

# MEDITATION

First ask yourself, "Why am I dating him [or her]? What need do I have that this person can fulfill?" If all your needs are financial or materialistic—these are blinders—that person cannot meet any spiritual needs. That person cannot pray you through. That person cannot encourage you to go to the next level in God. Has God sent him to help construct what He has already placed in your life, or has the devil sent him to destroy you?

(*No More Sheets*, Revised Edition, Page 116)

Are your relationships Spirit-led or needs-driven? What is the difference?
How do Spirit-led relationships differ from needs-driven ones?

---

# DAY 19

# Do It Right

*The blessing of the Lord, it maketh rich, and He addeth no sorrow with it. It is as sport to a fool to do mischief: but a man of understanding hath wisdom* (Proverbs 10:22-23).

# TODAY'S DEVOTION

How can you date someone whom your sister has dated? That's just not cool. Even before I got saved, I followed this principle: I never dated anyone my natural sister dated. In case you didn't know, it's taboo. I'm not speaking about your sister going out to dinner two or three times and discovering the guy wasn't her type. I have gone to dinner a few times and said, "I think my sister and you would be a better match."...

You need to assist the man who is your brother in the Lord before dating him. Make sure that he walks in integrity. Has he left any scars behind? Has he wounded anybody? While you're testifying how the Lord blessed you with a husband, some sister may be bleeding because he emotionally and mentally abused her. If a sister in the Body of Christ has already dated a brother and you're interested in him, you must do some research. Whether you have a casual or close relationship with her, you need to talk. Asking a few questions could save you some big problems.

(*No More Sheets*, Revised Edition, Page 118)

# CHALLENGE THE SHEETS

1. A dating relationship should be a blessing all around. I shared my rules about dating a sister's ex-boyfriend. What are some dating situations that you make a point to avoid? Describe a sticky situation you wish you had avoided.

_____

_____

_____

_____

_____

_____

_____

_____

2. In the 21st century, many societal rules are seen as being quaint. The taboo of dating the same guy your sister dated is taboo for a reason. If you do not resist this temptation, what might be the consequences?

_____

_____

_____

_____

_____

_____

_____

_____

_____

3. You need to know the history of the person you're dating. Consider a past relationship in which you failed to do the research. What unexpected consequence did you face as a result? What big headaches might a little bit of research have averted?

_____

_____

_____

_____

_____

_____

4. Are you dating someone who has left scars on someone else? What do those scars tell you?

_____

_____

_____

_____

_____

_____

5. What can you learn from the person who suffered those scars? What is the value—to the person and to you—of reaching out in this way?

_____

_____

_____

_____

_____

_____

# MEDITATION

When you know or even think a sister may have been sexually involved with a man, don't date him. Or, if a sister has dated him for more than six months, then you two women need to talk. She must be allowed to say, "I see that you have an interest in this brother. We went out a couple of times. We both agreed that this is not the will of God for our lives. I don't want you to think that there is any emotional attachment between us." There is a right and wrong way to do everything.

(*No More Sheets*, Revised Edition, Page 118)

> The right way of doing something is not always the easiest. How does getting the above situations right create a strong foundation for a new relationship?

_____

_____

_____

_____

_____

_____

_____

_____

_____

_____

_____

_____

_____

_____

_____

# Rinse Away the Residue

*Better is the poor that walketh in his integrity, than he that is perverse in his lips, and is a fool. Also, that the soul be without knowledge, it is not good; and he that hasteth with his feet sinneth* (Proverbs 19:1-2).

# TODAY'S DEVOTION

I got on a plane one day and a man asked me if I would like to be a call girl, making $700 a call. Now get this, because this is powerful: What made him ask me that? Simply put, the residue of that old spirit was still on me. He was a Caucasian guy who did not know me from Adam. He told me that he had been watching me during the flight. His supervisor had asked him to find someone, and I looked like a person who might be interested. He told me that they worked out of downtown Manhattan. ... The girls and guys that worked for the organization entertained very wealthy people. He asked again would I like to become a professional call girl. He told me that they would buy all of my outfits, and I would live in a penthouse with them.

Now, I ask again: What would make him ask a saved, sanctified, Holy Spirit-filled girl like me a question like that? He saw the residue on me.... It was another chief [or spirit] who knew the spirit that was on me. That was the Lord's way of saying that I was not completely cleansed yet.

(*No More Sheets*, Revised Edition, Pages 133-134)

# CHALLENGE THE SHEETS

1. Being in the sheets leaves a spiritual mark that can be seen by other people who bear a similar mark. What does the story of the man on the plane say about the difference between someone's outward appearance and inward spiritual one?

_____

_____

_____

_____

_____

_____

_____

_____

2. Have you ever wondered why certain kinds of people are attracted to you? What does their attraction reveal about how you are being perceived in the spirit realm?

_____

_____

_____

_____

_____

_____

_____

_____

_____

_____

3. When you are dealing with low self-esteem and a chronic state of insufficient funds, the wrong people can make the wrong offers sound right for the wrong reasons. The offer on the plane was extreme, but even dating someone for their money is a bad idea. Consider your choices in this area. To what degree have you resisted this temptation? To what degree have you succumbed to it?

_____

_____

_____

_____

_____

4. The patterns in our lives are revealing *if* we pay attention to them. Are there any recurring relational patterns that reveal a spiritual "residue" of some kind? Explain.

_____

_____

_____

_____

_____

5. Sanctification is a lifelong process; there is always another level of spiritual cleansing ahead. Taking a snapshot of your life right now, is there an area of woundedness, scarring, or outright sin waiting to be cleansed? Explain.

_____

_____

_____

_____

_____

# MEDITATION

I was not completely cleansed yet.... I had gotten rid of all the boyfriends and phone numbers. I was even willing to walk in poverty, but I needed to be in a ministry that preached and operated in deliverance so that the spirit could be cast off me. It was still hovering around me, and I needed to be a part of a ministry that could break that filthy residue off of me. The anointing had to be heavy enough to go to the depths of my spirit and get the root, because if we don't get the root, it will grow back again.

(*No More Sheets*, Revised Edition, Page 134)

> To leave the sheets *and* the residue behind, you have to make the right choices and be under the right anointing. Are you involved in a ministry that can help you to break off any unclean residue?

# It Is Your Turn

*And we know that all things work together for good to them that love God, to them who are the called according to His purpose* (Romans 8:28).

# TODAY'S DEVOTION

You aren't reading this book by chance.... You're reading this book because it's your season; it's your turn. God is not going to leave you exposed to the enemy. He doesn't want you to be wandering in the wilderness, open prey for the crafty one. Your life doesn't have to be devoured.

...There's a story behind your life. There's a plan that God has for you. Right now, the Lord is earmarking people and destinations where you are going to be birthed into the fullness of your calling. Your miracle is going to come to pass. You will know [your church] home when you get there. You will know your shepherd when you see him. You will know the voice of God when you hear it. I prophesy to you right now, "The Lord is in control of your life. Fear not. What the enemy meant for your harm, the Lord is turning around for your good."...

*All things* work together for good. Every detail of your life fits into God's eternal plan.

(*No More Sheets*, Revised Edition, Pages 137-139)

# CHALLENGE THE SHEETS

1.  There are no accidents in God's Kingdom. Consider a current circumstance in your life and write a sentence or two about how God might use it for good.

_____

_____

_____

_____

_____

_____

_____

_____

_____

_____

2.  God always desires to protect you from the enemy. What is one way in which you can cooperate with His protection more fully?

_____

_____

_____

_____

_____

_____

_____

_____

_____

_____

3. Are any parts of your life being devoured? How does it help to be in the right church home? If you are in that church home, are you engaging with your leadership to your fullest advantage and the fullness of God's desire for you?

_____

_____

_____

_____

_____

4. What will the fullness of your calling look like? What is one step you can take today to move toward it? Are you aligning yourself with people who can help you or with people who will hold you back? Explain.

_____

_____

_____

_____

_____

5. We find it easy to say, "God is in control," and find it difficult to live as though He really is. How has God's ultimate control been demonstrated in your difficult times? In what areas have you tried to be the one in control? How so?

_____

_____

_____

_____

_____

# MEDITATION

If God has a destiny for your life, shouldn't you begin to prepare for it? Once you crawl out of the sheets, you'll find a lot more work to do. Yes, it's a big job. Yes, it requires faith and sacrifice. But if you make room for the Master, your life will never be the same.... Every detail of your life will work together for your good.

(*No More Sheets*, Revised Edition, Page 139)

> Has part of your destiny been on hold? If you make room for the Master today, how do you see that destiny unfolding?

# Purified and Purged

*But who may abide the day of His coming? and who shall stand when He appeareth? for He is like a refiner's fire, and like fullers' soap: and He shall sit as a refiner and purifier of silver: and He shall purify the sons of Levi, and purge them as gold and silver, that they may offer unto the Lord an offering in righteousness* (Malachi 3:2-3).

## Today's Devotion

The difference between the words *purify* and *purge* is powerful. Purify means "to make clean," but the word purge means to cleanse harshly.[1] God was letting me know back then that when He enters in, I must get rid of every connection to sin. When the Lord comes back in, He is going to purify me and make me clean, but this time it is going to be a harsh purging. (Please bear with me because I am going to feel the pain of this coming out.)

He was letting me know that there are really going to be some lonely days and very lonely nights. There will be some travailing. There must be a time of prayer and much Scripture reading. There must be much time spent in church. While in church during worship service, you will feel the residue lifting off of you. In other words, this will be a process.

An apt prayer is…Cleanse me, O Lord, and give me a new start.

(*No More Sheets,* Revised Edition, Pages 142-143)

# CHALLENGE THE SHEETS

1. What happens when precious metals are purified? What does the passage from Malachi reveal about God's presence and our spiritual state?

_____

_____

_____

_____

_____

_____

_____

_____

_____

_____

2. To be purged (cleansed harshly) sounds like an unattractive option, yet Scripture reveals that it is for our good. What do you stand to lose by avoiding God's purging?

_____

_____

_____

_____

_____

_____

_____

_____

_____

3. What can God do in you during the lonely days and nights of purging? How will He sustain you in that season?

_____

_____

_____

_____

_____

_____

4. Why are prayer, Scripture reading, and church attendance especially important during a season of purification and purging?

_____

_____

_____

_____

_____

_____

5. Purification and purging are not events, but processes. Why is this distinction important? How will understanding it help to sustain you in difficult times?

_____

_____

_____

_____

_____

_____

# MEDITATION

Purification and purging will not feel good. But just as a woman goes through pain while having a baby and the result of the pain makes her so very happy, so will it be with you. You will be able to say, "I am in pain, but I am in pain because I am being delivered. I am emptying out all of the junk that the enemy has put inside of me. I am emptying out all the sheets that were left in me. I am being washed with the fuller's soap—a very strong soap used in Biblical days. The Spirit of God is purifying me. I am being purged by the Holy Spirit."

(*No More Sheets*, Revised Edition, Page 142)

We often say, "No pain, no gain." How willing are you to endure the pain of being cleansed of any junk the enemy has brought into your life? What gain will result?

_____

_____

_____

_____

_____

_____

_____

_____

_____

_____

## ENDNOTE

1. Dictionary.com. s.v. "Purify"; s.v. "purge." http://dictionary.reference. com/browse/purify and http://dictionary.reference.com/browse/ purge; accessed January 04, 2010.

# Refined in Grace

*Wherein in time past ye walked according to the course of this world, according to the prince of the power of the air, the spirit that now worketh in the children of disobedience: among whom also we all had our conversation in times past in the lusts of our flesh, fulfilling the desires of the flesh and of the mind; and were by nature the children of wrath, even as others. But God, who is rich in mercy, for His great love wherewith He loved us, even when we were dead in sins, hath quickened us together with Christ...by grace ye are saved...* (Ephesians 2:2-5).

# Today's Devotion

Malachi 3:1 talks about the messenger who will come.... The messenger is the trainer...the refiner. ... The trainer will come and he will begin to *teach your spirit*.... The Lord will begin to tell you things. The Spirit of the Lord in your belly will convict you and will tell you, "Take it off. That's too short. That's too low. That's too sexy. That's too appealing. That's not of Me." It takes you going through this process to be able to hear the voice of God. Your flesh has a loud voice; it's got a big mouth. It doesn't want to die anyway.

The average person who gets saved wants to continue to do as many things as they used to and still profess salvation! When you've lived a life of sin, you must come *all* the way out. You are not a person who can live a borderline life. You are not a person who can take a chance. When you know you have a problem with your flesh, you can't test the waters. You cannot afford to live a borderline life.

(*No More Sheets*, Revised Edition, Pages 145-146)

# CHALLENGE THE SHEETS

1. By grace, we are delivered from the slavery of sin; but we still must make choices. How are our choices to be guided?

_____

_____

_____

_____

_____

_____

_____

_____

_____

_____

2. How will a life of prayer and supplication help to train you for godly living? How will it help you to hear God's voice?

_____

_____

_____

_____

_____

_____

_____

_____

_____

3. How do your responses to God's instruction position you to silence your flesh and amplify the voice of God?

_____

_____

_____

_____

_____

_____

4. How can the faith that brought you to salvation help you to abandon a harmful way of life? How will the grace by which you were saved enable you to resist sin in the days, months, and years to come?

_____

_____

_____

_____

_____

_____

5. What is it about sin that makes living a borderline life so dangerous?

_____

_____

_____

_____

_____

_____

# MEDITATION

A person who smokes can't visit a tobacco factory. A person who has an alcohol problem can't go to a wine-tasting event. Forget about it; *that's your chief.* You have to stay away from the atmosphere your chief lives in.

If your chief is sex, then you have to come away from porn movies to get that spirit off you. You can't sit and watch television—where people are putting their tongues down one another's throats—and think you're going to survive.... When satan's devices are at work, refuse to be used by them. Even when you feel weak, God is there.

(*No More Sheets,* Revised Edition, Pages 146-147)

> What environments are you choosing to enter? Are they helping you
> to reach your God-given destiny or keeping you stuck in the past?
> How so?

_____

_____

_____

_____

_____

_____

_____

_____

_____

_____

_____

_____

# You Can Change Your Destiny

*And I will rebuke the devourer for your sakes, and he shall not destroy the fruits of your ground; neither shall your vine cast her fruit before the time in the field, saith the Lord of hosts. And all nations shall call you blessed: for ye shall be a delightsome land, saith the Lord of hosts* (Malachi 3:11-12).

# TODAY'S DEVOTION

You can change your destiny.... There is a process which God intends for you to follow.... If you do it His way, you're going to be blessed; but if you do it any other way, you will surely be cursed. After you've gone through His process, then other aspects of your life will fall into place. There are things in your character that will begin to reflect the manifestation of the process.

Let me give you an example of what I'm trying to say. There are people who have received titles in the Church and find themselves pressed for people to respect their title. When what is manifesting in your character is not appropriate with your title, people will call you what they see.

As I began to yield to the purification and the purging of the Holy Spirit, people automatically began to call me Evangelist Bynum or Prophetess Bynum. I didn't have to say, "Excuse me. Don't disrespect me by calling me Juanita." You don't demand honor. Honor is given when the manifestation of that honor is operating in you. The Bible says that after you go through the process, nations will call you blessed. Your name will change and they will recognize your calling.

(*No More Sheets,* Revised Edition, Page 153)

# CHALLENGE THE SHEETS

1. Reflect on Malachi 3:11-12. How has the devourer impacted your life? What forms of restoration do you need to begin to change your destiny?

_____

_____

_____

_____

_____

_____

_____

_____

_____

_____

2. In your own words, what does it mean to be blessed? Cursed? Do you see evidence of blessing in your life? Of cursing? Explain.

_____

_____

_____

_____

_____

_____

_____

_____

_____

_____

3. Which areas of your character most reflect God's ways? Which areas are most in need of God's process? How will growth in character help the other pieces of your life to fall into place? Be specific.

_____

_____

_____

_____

_____

4. Do people automatically recognize your calling? What specific elements in your character and lifestyle contribute to their ability to recognize your calling?

_____

_____

_____

_____

_____

5. In what specific ways is honor being demonstrated through your life? How is honor returned to you by others? Is there room for growth in this area? How so?

_____

_____

_____

_____

_____

_____

# MEDITATION

You cannot live in sin for ten years and want to walk in God with a mere piece of a Sunday morning message and think you're going to survive. You have to be processed back into your divine state. You gave the devil time to process you out of your divine state. Now, you must give God the same amount of years to process you back to Him.

You have no legal right to say that the Word doesn't work until you have given it the same amount of time that you gave sin!... You've *got* to get all that cleaned out! That is a harsh cleansing. Whatever you present to God after this point, it is done in righteousness—whether it be money or whether it be serving in the Church.

(*No More Sheets*, Revised Edition, Page 154)

> How committed are you to God's cleansing process? Are you willing to be patient with yourself as He works to restore you to your divine state? Will you allow Him to love you in the process?

# Respect Your Body

*Who changed the truth of God into a lie, and worshipped and served the creature more than the Creator, who is blessed for ever. Amen. For this cause God gave them up unto vile affections: for even their women did change the natural use into that which is against nature: and likewise also the men, leaving the natural use of the woman, burned in their lust one toward another; men with men working that which is unseemly, and receiving in themselves that recompence of their error which was meet* (Romans 1:25-27).

# Today's Devotion

You are in a battle to regain the respect of your body.... If you will not respect God, then you will not have respect for your body. Likewise, you are not going to have respect for anyone else, nor anyone else's body. The Word teaches [in Romans 1:25-27], "I'm going to cause you to dishonor your body, because you didn't honor My body."...

Those whom God gave up became lesbians and homosexuals. The women and men went against nature. Women had no more need for the law of the creation.

The Bible always requires that the male leave his father and his mother and cleave to his wife (see Gen. 2:24). However, due to their own foolishness, the men left the natural use of a woman. This was the total opposite of the instruction from God. The Lord's instructions were to leave mother and father. He didn't say leave women.

The beginning of man's destruction is when he started walking in rebellion to what the will of the Father was. But here, because of his own imagination and his lack of respect to the body of God, men began to leave the women and burn in lust one toward another.

(*No More Sheets*, Revised Edition, Pages 161-162)

# CHALLENGE THE SHEETS

1. Explain what happens when we worship and serve the creature more than the Creator (see Rom. 1:25). Why is this so?

_____

_____

_____

_____

_____

_____

_____

_____

_____

_____

2. When we choose the sheets, we disrespect our own bodies. Explain how this reflects the degree to which we respect God.

_____

_____

_____

_____

_____

_____

_____

_____

_____

3. Consider today's shifting sexual attitudes in light of Romans 1:25-27. How do current-day rationales for homosexuality compare with Paul's explanation of the root of sexual perversion? Do those who present these rationales honor and respect their own bodies?

_____

_____

_____

_____

_____

4. Read Hosea 4:6. Has a lack of knowledge caused you to disrespect your own body? How has your understanding changed and how will your choices change as a result?

_____

_____

_____

_____

_____

5. Often, we know what God's will is and we rebel against Him. What role has rebellion played in your relationships? What price has been paid for your rebellion?

_____

_____

_____

_____

_____

# MEDITATION

We are going to know God by gaining the knowledge of the way He created us. The wife receives a deposit from the husband which produces a child. This is the reason the Bible calls the plan of salvation being born again.

You may say, "My grandma was a nymphomaniac. My daddy was a whoremonger along with all of my uncles. It's just in my blood." But upon receiving a blood transfusion from the blood of Jesus Christ, old things have passed away; behold, all things—my blood system, my heritage, the way I look, the way I talk, the way I act—are become new (see 2 Cor. 5:17).

Apply the blood of the Lamb to the doorposts of your heart. The death that comes from sin and transgression will pass over your life.

(*No More Sheets*, Revised Edition, Page 163)

> Once you have received the "deposit" of the blood of Jesus Christ you are reborn. Write a short note that tells the story of how being born again has transformed your "bloodline" and redeemed you from any negative inherited traits.

_____

_____

_____

_____

_____

_____

_____

_____

_____

# Put on the "New Man"

*But ye have not so learned Christ; if so be that ye have heard Him, and have been taught by Him, as the truth is in Jesus: that ye put off concerning the former conversation the old man, which is corrupt according to the deceitful lusts; and be renewed in the spirit of your mind; and that ye put on the new man, which after God is created in righteousness and true holiness. Wherefore putting away lying, speak every man truth with his neighbour: for we are members one of another (Ephesians 4:20-25).*

# Today's Devotion

Hear Him through His Word. The real truth is the Word. You have to put away the former conversation of the old man, which is corrupt according to the deceitful lust. From this knowledge, you will change how you talk and who you talk to. You might say, "I need a prophecy; I need a prophet." No—you need a Bible! Hear Him through His Word.

You have to cease from vain babbling and vain conversation. Why? Because your conversation will speak out of the residue of the lust of your flesh, which is not purified. You will begin to sit up and talk sex and junk. Put away the conversation of the old man and be renewed in the spirit of your mind. How does that happen? It happens through the Word.

This is the way you put on the new man: you put on the new man by searching for him through the Word. How is this man made? He is made after God, who *is* Righteousness and True Holiness. When you find truth in God's Word, it is a seed that is planted in your heart.

(*No More Sheets*, Revised Edition, Pages 167-168)

# CHALLENGE THE SHEETS

1. According to Ephesians 4:20-25, what are some of the ways in which you put off the "old man" and put on the new one?

_____

_____

_____

_____

_____

_____

_____

_____

_____

_____

2. The passage from Ephesians speaks of being "taught by Him." What is the primary way in which we hear from God?

_____

_____

_____

_____

_____

_____

_____

_____

_____

_____

3. When you are taught by God, what happens to your words? How are your relationships affected? Describe some ways in which you have seen this happen in your own life.

_____

_____

_____

_____

_____

_____

4. How does the residue of the lust of your flesh differ from the product of a renewed mind? In which areas of your life do you see the "residue" being replaced by "renewal"?

_____

_____

_____

_____

_____

_____

5. You plant the truth of God's Word in your heart. Think about the qualities of seed in a natural setting; what does this tell you about your potential for fruitfulness based on the Word you have planted?

_____

_____

_____

_____

_____

_____

# MEDITATION

You must be careful to protect your seed.... You must work on your life as a single person and get to know yourself all over again. *You must spend quality time with yourself....* You must learn your weaknesses and your strengths so that you are no longer deceived....

You can no longer afford to feed yourself junk.... We have all been designed and structured differently. Our levels of tolerance are different. You must learn that what your home girls may do, may not be something you can embrace and still live to tell the story. You must know yourself to the degree that you are able to look a situation in the face and determine that it's not for you. You must protect your purification and your position in God.

(*No More Sheets,* Revised Edition, Pages 168-169)

How well do you know *you?* Write a few short bullet points describing your likes and dislikes, weaknesses and strengths, and dreams for the future.

_____

_____

_____

_____

_____

_____

_____

_____

_____

_____

_____

_____

# Delivered and Justified

*And for this cause He is the mediator of the new testament, that by means of death, for the redemption of the transgressions that were under the first testament, they which are called might receive the promise of eternal inheritance. For where a testament is, there must also of necessity be the death of the testator. For a testament is of force after men are dead: otherwise it is of no strength at all while the testator liveth* (Hebrews 9:15-17).

# Today's Devotion

*Justification* means that you have been acquitted and the offenses of the sin in your life are erased as if you never did it. That means when you stand before God, there are no telltale signs that you used to be a lesbian or a homosexual. There is no proof that you used to smoke cigarettes or were a drug addict. When you walk in the full operation of justification, there should be no appearance of any part of your old lifestyle. In other words, it should be a secret unless you want to tell it....

Read today's passage from Hebrews again. There is a revelation in having a testimony. What makes a testimony have power is when there is a death of the testator. It gives him a testimony. He talks about what he died to and what he was resurrected into. If you die in it, it is buried and is no longer a part of you. Therefore, when you testify, you resurrect the memory of what God has done for you. That's why you have a testimony. When you have been saved two or three years, we should not be able to look at you and tell that you were a drug addict or a prostitute.

(*No More Sheets*, Revised Edition, Pages 171-172)

# CHALLENGE THE SHEETS

1. According to Hebrews 9:15-17, we have a testimony *because* Jesus, our Mediator, died. Take a moment and put into words your appreciation for all Jesus has done for you.

_____

_____

_____

_____

_____

_____

_____

_____

2. If Jesus is your Savior, your sins have been erased and God no longer remembers them. To what degree do you still condemn yourself? What does this say about the redemption Jesus purchased for you?

_____

_____

_____

_____

_____

_____

_____

_____

_____

3. When justification operates fully in your life, the signs of past sins disappear. Describe the transformation that is evident in your life so far. How does this change affect the way you feel about yourself? About God?

_____

_____

_____

_____

_____

4. Have you ever shared your testimony? How does the "burial" of sin give you the freedom to do so? How can your freedom affect those who hear your testimony?

_____

_____

_____

_____

5. Why is it important to "resurrect" the memory of what God has done for you? Apart from what it does for you and for others, how does it magnify God?

_____

_____

_____

_____

_____

# MEDITATION

When the people of old went out and told of the works of Jesus, people were convinced. Do you know why?... They saw the manifestation of miracles in the lives of those who witnessed about Him. Someone who has had problems in their walk with God can say, "I used to smoke two packs a day. I used to be a prostitute, but now I am justified." That's a gift that comes along with salvation. Justification makes you look as if you have never been a sinner. It makes you look as if you have never been a liar, a cheater, or a prisoner. You have been justified by the faith of Christ. Therefore, you have *peace* with God.

(*No More Sheets*, Revised Edition, Page 172)

> On a practical level, what does it mean to have peace with God? Are you enjoying the peace that comes from your having been justified or do you try, at times, to self-justify by your works? Is it possible to do both?

_____

_____

_____

_____

_____

_____

_____

_____

_____

_____

_____

_____

# Live on the Altar

*I beseech you therefore, brethren, by the mercies of God, that ye present your bodies a living sacrifice, holy, acceptable unto God, which is your reasonable service. And be not conformed to this world: but be ye transformed by the renewing of your mind, that ye may prove what is that good, and acceptable, and perfect, will of God* (Romans 12:1-2).

# Today's Devotion

*Sanctification* goes along with justification and regeneration. It means you no longer have to walk according to your natural family lineage, but you will be what your Father in Heaven is. Now that's *powerful!* This means you have been made to sit in right relationship to God's laws. You have been born again to a new life—bought with a price—therefore you are not your own person.

Sanctification means that you have been set aside to serve the Lord because He paid for you and you are owned by Him. *When He regenerated you, you were adopted into His house.* He went to the adoption agency, adopted you, and took you to His house. Once you get in His house—because you are so thankful that you're not in an orphanage anymore—you promise to serve Him. Serving Him doesn't mean nursing, ushering, or collecting the offering. Serving Him means that you have now become dedicated to the altar.

…Being *justified* says you belong to the righteous. Being *regenerated* says you are a child of God. Being *sanctified* says you are made holy. You are not born holy. You are made holy…. Deliverance is sometimes immediate, but sanctification is an ongoing process.

(*No More Sheets*, Revised Edition, Pages 173-175)

# CHALLENGE THE SHEETS

1. What does it mean, in real-life terms, to present your body as a living sacrifice? Give examples.

_____

_____

_____

_____

_____

_____

_____

_____

_____

_____

_____

2. What choices in your life demonstrate the belief that you are no longer your own? How do these choices differ from those you have made in the past?

_____

_____

_____

_____

_____

_____

_____

_____

_____

_____

3. How do your choices testify to the sanctification process? Are they impacting your habits? Your mindsets? How?

_____

_____

_____

_____

_____

_____

4. How do your answers to the previous three questions give definition to the idea of a life that is dedicated to the altar?

_____

_____

_____

_____

_____

_____

5. What does it mean to you to be adopted into God's family? How was your thinking different when you were a spiritual orphan?

_____

_____

_____

_____

_____

_____

_____

# MEDITATION

My dedication and my sanctification mean that I have been glued for eternity to the altar. I have dedicated myself to the point where I vow that I will serve Him until I die. A *saved* person is *one who has been set right with God, adopted in the divine family, and is now dedicated to God's service....*

I hear people say this a lot: "No one tells me whether I am saved or not. No one tells me how to dress." Well, maybe they don't, but your actions speak for you. The outward change called justification is followed by an inward change called regeneration; this, in turn, is followed by your dedication to God's service.

(*No More Sheets,* Revised Edition, Pages 174-175)

> Being delivered is only part of your testimony. Have you transitioned out of the sheets and onto the altar? Do you desire to present yourself on the altar? Why?

_____

_____

_____

_____

_____

_____

_____

_____

_____

_____

_____

_____

# Baptized With Fire

*And, behold, I send the promise of My Father upon you: but tarry ye in the city of Jerusalem, until ye be endued with power from on high* (Luke 24:49).

## Today's Devotion

The Bible says [in Acts 2:38] that you don't have to seek for the Holy Spirit for He is a gift.... The Holy Spirit first fell on believers on the day of Pentecost. The saints were in one accord in one place—the upper room. Jesus had sent them to a designated place—a place that was away from their family, phone, television, and junk.... He sent them among people whose desires were the same. They were all hungry for the Holy Spirit.

*"And when the day of Pentecost was fully come, they were all with one accord in one place"* (Acts 2:1). The Bible says that the Holy Spirit fell when they were all in one accord. Now what am I saying? We are body, soul, and spirit. Your body has to be submitted to the fact that your soul is hungry and thirsty for the Holy Spirit, and your spirit desires Him.

When body, soul, and spirit all get together in one place with one aim, the Holy Spirit will fall on you. The gift of the Holy Spirit will manifest Himself in you.

(*No More Sheets*, Revised Edition, Pages 176-177)

# CHALLENGE THE SHEETS

1. What is the difference between a gift and something you must earn? How do you respond to each?

_____

_____

_____

_____

_____

_____

_____

_____

_____

2. Acts 2:38 refers to *"the gift of the Holy Ghost."* Romans 5 refers to the gift of salvation. What is God's purpose in giving salvation and the Holy Spirit as gifts rather than as rewards to be earned?

_____

_____

_____

_____

_____

_____

_____

_____

_____

_____

3. Why did Jesus send His disciples to a designated place to receive the Holy Spirit? How did this affect events on the Day of Pentecost? How did it affect the Church for the long term?

_____

_____

_____

_____

_____

4. Why was being in one accord so important on the Day of Pentecost? Why is it important to the Church today?

_____

_____

_____

_____

_____

5. How does the unity of your body, soul, and spirit affect your interaction with the Holy Spirit?

_____

_____

_____

_____

_____

_____

# MEDITATION

*"The Comforter, which is the Holy Ghost, whom the Father will send in My name, He shall teach you all things, and bring all things to your remembrance, whatsoever I have said unto you"* (John 14:26).

The Bible says that the Holy Ghost is a teacher.... There is a voice in the depths of your soul and it's talking to you. It is leading and guiding you. There's an unction that comes up and tells you don't do this, or don't do that, put that down, don't touch that, don't go here, turn that off, don't watch that, and don't taste that. This is a true manifestation. The Holy Spirit does not only come in, but here is where He *resides.*

(*No More Sheets*, Revised Edition, Page 177)

> Have you heard the voice of the Holy Spirit today and, if not, have you invited Him to speak into your life? How eager are you to hear from Him? Why?

_____

_____

_____

_____

_____

_____

_____

_____

_____

_____

_____

_____

_____

_____

# Mastered by Masturbation?

*Casting down imaginations, and every high thing that exalteth itself against the knowledge of God, and bringing into captivity every thought to the obedience of Christ...* (2 Corinthians 10:5).

## TODAY'S DEVOTION

Through my own experience, I have understood that a clear definition of masturbation is the bait that satan uses to become a master of you! This spirit forces you to relive past sexual relationships or future fantasies. And what happens is this: When the physical sensation is over, the pain of the reality is now in your face. That's when you realize that the hurt has not healed.

Hear this: Many times people feel that when they masturbate, it's just a physical exercise. That is a far cry from being the truth because when you indulge in this act, you actually have to go into the spirit of your mind. This is why the Bible says to be renewed by the spirit of your mind.

In the seat of the spirit of your mind—where the imagination of the Lord does not reside and where impure thoughts are—there is the evil working of the enemy in the thought realm. When you travel into that realm to such a depth that you cause a physical sensation, you have tampered with demons in a realm that you know not of.

When you masturbate, you are allowing a spirit to arouse you. Your spirit is wide open and you don't know what spirit of perversion has jumped inside you.

(*No More Sheets,* Revised Edition, Pages 181-182)

# CHALLENGE THE SHEETS

1. How does masturbation amount to the exaltation of imaginations and other high things against the knowledge of God?

_____

_____

_____

_____

_____

_____

_____

_____

_____

2. How do you feel (not physically, but emotionally) after masturbating? How do these feelings reveal the truth that masturbation is not God's idea?

_____

_____

_____

_____

_____

_____

_____

_____

_____

3. Where does your imagination travel during masturbation? Explain how your answer supports the idea that masturbation is more than a physical exercise.

_____

_____

_____

_____

_____

_____

_____

4. How does masturbation serve to cover up unmet needs and unresolved spiritual issues where sex and relationships are concerned?

_____

_____

_____

_____

_____

5. Consider the demonic activity that masturbation invites. Are you aware of the toll it is taking? Ask God to reveal the signs of this activity. Then repent of it and receive His healing.

_____

_____

_____

_____

_____

_____

_____

# MEDITATION

Let me just say this: The trips and the journeys that you go through in your mind to reach an orgasm is what the Bible means when it says casting down imaginations and every high thing that exalts itself against, against, against the proper method of doing things. And the proper method of doing things is doing them in the knowledge of God....

When you reach an orgasm from the realm of imagination, you have traveled into the spirit realm for that climax. You are out of control, your body is responding to that act, and you don't know what spirits from that realm have entered you....

Don't even fool yourself. Masturbation and pornography will never be enough to satisfy you.

(*No More Sheets,* Revised Edition, Pages 185-186)

> Are you allowing the knowledge of God to reign over your ideas about your needs, desires, and sexual destiny? How can His truth replace your perceived need for sexual gratification through masturbation?

---
---
---
---
---
---
---
---
---
---

# Arrest Sin's Conception

*Blessed is the man that endureth temptation: for when he is tried, he shall receive the crown of life, which the Lord hath promised to them that love Him. Let no man say when he is tempted, I am tempted of God: for God cannot be tempted with evil, neither tempteth He any man: but every man is tempted, when he is drawn away of his own lust, and enticed. Then when lust hath conceived, it bringeth forth sin: and sin, when it is finished, bringeth forth death* (James 1:12-15).

# Today's Devotion

When you return to things that are ungodly, you are returning to what is still in your soul. This is where you experience what the Bible calls backsliding. It's like pushing the reverse button and taking your life back to the era when you did not know God. Let's properly describe masturbation: It's like eating vomit. Proverbs 26:11 says, *"As a dog returneth to his vomit, so a fool returneth to his folly."*...

You may be asking this question: Why is it that some spirits can just come out, but it takes others *so* long? Well, the answer is simple. When the Spirit of God first started calling you away or warning you not to walk into that trap, you ignored the voice of God and the Word of God. So now that you have been forgiven, you walk in a penalty for the rebellion.

Don't let anybody tell you differently. God forgives you, but there is a penalty you pay for rebellion—even if it's mental warfare. The mind must be completely renewed and the flesh retrained. But I'm your witness—the closer you get to God and the more you stay in His Word, the quicker you come out.

(*No More Sheets*, Revised Edition, Page 194)

# CHALLENGE THE SHEETS

1. Bad habits are hard to break. How does a return to the "vomit" of masturbation or any bad habit reveal the content of your soul?

_____

_____

_____

_____

_____

_____

_____

_____

2. Yesterday, we discussed the demonic spirits involved in masturbation. How does the repeated "invitation" of masturbation contribute to these spirits' stubbornness in sticking around? How can you "revoke" your invitation?

_____

_____

_____

_____

_____

_____

_____

_____

_____

3. When did your conscience first inform you that masturbation was the wrong thing to do? What were the signals God gave you? Did you ignore the signals? What was your rationale at the time?

_____

_____

_____

_____

_____

4. God forgives, but sin has consequences. What have been the effects of masturbation in your life overall? What kinds of entanglements has it brought to your mind?

_____

_____

_____

_____

_____

5. Are you committed to being set free in this area? What role does the Word of God play in your deliverance? How will prayer help you to draw closer to God and to freedom?

_____

_____

_____

_____

_____

# MEDITATION

Lust is an insatiable spirit and an unappeasable work of the flesh. Once lust has conceived—meaning that you have wished in your heart that you could get involved in sexual immorality again—then you've allowed the seed to be planted, and it has already begun to grow. Lust that's been conceived brings forth sin. If you receive what the Word of God is saying, you will live, but if you reject what God's Word is saying, you will be drawn away. The Word states to us that the wages that sin pays is death, but the gift that God gives, which is the plan of salvation, is eternal life! (See Romans 6:23.)

(*No More Sheets*, Revised Edition, Page 197)

> James 1:12-15 explains how lust is conceived. How can walking in the Word and waiting on the Lord empower you to prevent the conception of this sin?

_____

_____

_____

_____

_____

_____

_____

_____

_____

_____

_____

_____

_____

# DAY 32

# Power in Thinking

*Finally, brethren, whatsoever things are true, whatsoever things are honest, whatsoever things are just, whatsoever things are pure, whatsoever things are lovely, whatsoever things are of good report; if there be any virtue, and if there be any praise, think on these things. Those things, which ye have both learned, and received, and heard, and seen in me, do: and the God of peace shall be with you* (Philippians 4:8-9).

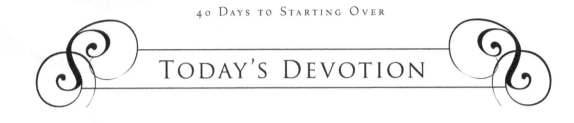

# Today's Devotion

Philippians 2:5 says, *"Let this mind be in you, which was also in Christ Jesus...."* So you may ask yourself, "Then what should I think on?" Philippians 4:8-9 has the answer:... Those things that you've learned, seen, and heard of the Lord...think on those things. *"For as* [you] *thinketh in* [your] *heart, so* [are you]*..."* (Proverbs 23:7).

Wherever you put your concentration and your focus, that is what you become. So the deception of the enemy is to keep you thinking about things in your mind that are impure—things that have no good report, things that are not just, and things that are not filled with virtue—so that you don't become those godly things. He wants you to think of all the ungodly things because the more ungodliness you think about, the more ungodly you become. The more you think on things pertaining to the things of God, the more like God you become.

This is why we must make sure that our thoughts line up with who Christ says we are. We must take that thought and say, "satan, I rebuke you in Jesus' name. I cast this thing out of my mind. I am operating with a pure mind and pure thoughts and according to the Word of God. I am going to let the mind of Christ be in me."

(*No More Sheets*, Revised Edition, Pages 198-199)

# CHALLENGE THE SHEETS

1. Your thoughts are powerful! How have thoughts and thought patterns influenced your life up to this point? Are you satisfied with the direction your thoughts have dictated?

_____

_____

_____

_____

_____

_____

_____

_____

2. Sometimes it is easier to see how certain principles are working in someone else's life. Can you think of someone whose thoughts and beliefs have led to godly outcomes? Explain.

_____

_____

_____

_____

_____

_____

_____

_____

_____

3. How can you be helped by the example or mentoring of someone whose thoughts have led to godly outcomes? Are you willing to pay the price they paid in terms of self-discipline and determination?

_____

_____

_____

_____

_____

4. How successful has the enemy been in distracting you with ungodly thoughts? How have his distractions affected your emotions? Your outcomes? How can God's instruction from Philippians 4:8-9 help you to turn the tables on the enemy?

_____

_____

_____

_____

_____

5. List three distorted beliefs about yourself that the enemy has used to entrap you in ungodliness (i.e., I'm not smart enough to succeed in life; I'm not attractive and must settle for less than God's best in my relationships; I am afraid to be alone; therefore I will give into sinful sexual demands to keep my man/woman). What does God's Word say to refute these lies?

_____

_____

_____

_____

# MEDITATION

Anything contrary to the will of God must be cast down, whether it be ideologies, doctrines, traditions, or ways in which we were raised. Remember, the enemy is not going to stop tempting you. Never, never, never! He wants back in, and the only way to get in is to tempt and entice. First he says, "I must get the appetite so strong that the desire becomes overwhelming, until they can't resist." So you must not think badly about yourself because you are tempted. You are supposed to be tempted. Temptation is not wrong. Yielding to temptation is wrong.

(*No More Sheets*, Revised Edition, Page 200)

> Thinking God's thoughts *will* change your life for the better! Think about the ideologies, doctrines, traditions, or childhood experiences that need to be dethroned and replaced with God's thoughts and ways. Is God's plan for your life becoming clearer?

_____

_____

_____

_____

_____

_____

_____

_____

_____

_____

_____

_____

# DAY 33

# Junk in, Junk Out

*My son, attend to My words; incline thine ear unto My sayings. Let them not depart from thine eyes; keep them in the midst of thine heart. For they are life unto those that find them, and health to all their flesh. Keep thy heart with all diligence; for out of it are the issues of life. Put away from thee a froward mouth, and perverse lips put far from thee. Let thine eyes look right on, and let thine eyelids look straight before thee. Ponder the path of thy feet, and let all thy ways be established. Turn not to the right hand nor to the left: remove thy foot from evil* (Proverbs 4:20-27).

# Today's Devotion

We have a lower nature that is influenced by the spirit of this world. I want to give you a revelation from the Word that will set you free. You're getting ready to realize that you are what the Word says you are. Your days of being subjected to the enemy and the tactics of this world are over. From this day forward, you will know that if you are enslaved, it's because you want to be and not because you have to be.

Proverbs 4:20-27 reveals that you have to *guard* what enters into your eyes and ears and definitely what comes out of your mouth! If you allow satanic things to enter into your ears and your eyes, you may not have actually performed the act, but it will influence you to operate according to what you have seen and heard....

When you play around by saying things like "I sure would like to be with him," the enemy will get a hold of your joke and turn it into reality. That will lead your spirit down the wrong path and cause you to fall into sexual sin. Don't have wandering eyes.

(*No More Sheets*, Revised Edition, Pages 204-205)

# CHALLENGE THE SHEETS

1. In Proverbs 4:20-27, Solomon warns us to guard what goes into our hearts. What does he say comes out of your heart that makes your intake so important?

_____

_____

_____

_____

_____

_____

_____

_____

2. What is your primary source for knowing who you *really* are? Why is knowing this so important when it comes to guarding your heart?

_____

_____

_____

_____

_____

_____

_____

_____

3. Explain how enslavement is a choice. How can you choose freedom instead?

_____

_____

_____

_____

_____

_____

4. How are your thinking and speaking as powerful as the things you actually do? How does this work in your favor? How can it work against you?

_____

_____

_____

_____

_____

_____

5. What are the dangers of joking around about things that are contrary to God's will for your life? What does a joke reveal about the intent of your heart?

_____

_____

_____

_____

_____

_____

# MEDITATION

Guard your heart.... Remember, if the enemy can't bring a person to seduce you, he will still seduce you by what you hear and what you look at. If you want to recover from that sickness, you have to incline your ear to the Word of God. If what you hear and see is coming from the Word, then it will keep you.... From this day forward, you will know that if you are enslaved, it's because you want to be, not because you have to be.

(*No More Sheets*, Revised Edition, Pages 204-205)

Have you given the enemy the "key" to your heart? How can you secure the gates of your heart against his schemes? How can you make your heart more open to God?

_____

_____

_____

_____

_____

_____

_____

_____

_____

_____

_____

_____

_____

_____

_____

_____

# Kill the "Chief"

*The Lord is my shepherd; I shall not want. He maketh me to lie down in green pastures: He leadeth me beside the still waters. He restoreth my soul: He leadeth me in the paths of righteousness for His name's sake. Yea, though I walk through the valley of the shadow of death, I will fear no evil: for Thou art with me; Thy rod and Thy staff they comfort me (Psalms 23:1-4).*

## TODAY'S DEVOTION

...Submission has become such a problem in our everyday lives. We have not yet been able to recognize, even as single people, the power of our leadership....

We need to understand that there are three responsibilities based on three different entities: personal responsibility, pastoral responsibility, and God's responsibility. God would never assume our responsibilities, and we could never handle His responsibilities. Neither can we handle the responsibilities of our pastors, or they ours.

Now, I honestly believe that, in combination, all three bring about complete deliverance for an individual who is trying to walk out of sexual sin. What brought me to that conclusion is this: Of all the times that I struggled on my own to walk that thing out—when I didn't have a shepherd protecting me—I failed. It is a known fact that after a sheep walks so many feet away from his shepherd, he's immediately blind. The Bible constantly refers back to that fact [as Psalms 23:1-4 shows].

(*No More Sheets*, Revised Edition, Pages 209-210)

# CHALLENGE THE SHEETS

1. As the Body of Christ, we need one another. Describe a situation in which God used your church leadership to speak into your life or protect you from spiritual harm.

_____

_____

_____

_____

_____

_____

_____

2. In the context of your relationships with the opposite sex and deliverance from the sheets, name two areas of your personal responsibility (specific choices or actions that are within your power to control). Are you satisfied that you are fulfilling your responsibilities? Is there room for improvement in either area? Explain.

_____

_____

_____

_____

_____

_____

_____

_____

3. What responsibilities do your leaders have in regard to your overall spiritual health and your deliverance from the sheets? How can you enable them to fulfill their responsibilities?

_____

_____

_____

_____

_____

4. As your heavenly Father, God is committed to your deliverance. Based on Scripture, what is God's role in your deliverance? To what degree have you invited Him into this area of your life? How might you be more open to His work in you?

_____

_____

_____

_____

_____

5. Are there any areas in which you have attempted to fulfill the role assigned to God or your leaders? Explain what these areas are, and describe your results.

_____

_____

_____

_____

_____

_____

# MEDITATION

Now the same nature that God the Shepherd has, the pastor as shepherd has. If the pastor you are now sitting under cannot lead you beside still waters, restore your soul, and help you fear no evil when you walk through a valley experience, there is a problem....

Your pastor has the weapons it takes to sneak up on the enemy. If you've had a problem with submission, then the enemy is not expecting you to have leadership. He's not expecting anybody to be covering you and praying for you. Now, you by yourself may not be able to defend the enemy. But you, being covered in prayer and covered by a shepherd, have already won the battle.

(*No More Sheets*, Revised Edition, Pages 210, 212)

> If you have a church, get to know your pastors. Seek the guidance you
> need when you need it. If you don't yet have a church, trust God to lead
> you to the right one.

# Single and Whole

*Favour is deceitful, and beauty is vain: but a woman that feareth the Lord, she shall be praised. Give her of the fruit of her hands; and let her own works praise her in the gates* (Proverbs 31:30-31).

## Today's Devotion

Have you ever wondered why you're not married? You're not married because you're not single yet.... If you expect God to bring a mate to you, you must get purged of certain ideas: "I'm looking for a mate to satisfy all of my needs. I'm on welfare now, but when my husband comes, he's going to change all that. I'm impressed by all the things this man has—all the things he can buy me."

Buy your own furniture, flowers, television, DVD, and car. Then, when he comes, you will be able to make a conscious decision about his character. You won't allow what he has to blind you to the man he really is. This will leave you with enough room to make the right decision.

Women, it is high time that you realize that sheets are expensive. They will cost you your mind. The mind of a powerful woman is a terrible thing to waste. You've got to be busy at your goals. If you are a woman who has not yet set goals for yourself, or if you don't know what road to take, then any road will do. You have to have goals so that you can occupy yourself with your dreams.

(*No More Sheets*, Revised Edition, Pages 221-222)

# CHALLENGE THE SHEETS

1. A single woman (or man) can be as industrious as the woman described in Proverbs 31. Are you single and living, or single and waiting to live?

_____

_____

_____

_____

_____

_____

_____

_____

_____

2. Do you have any single-and-waiting-to-live mindsets that need to be shed? How do they impede your progress and limit your development?

_____

_____

_____

_____

_____

_____

_____

_____

_____

_____

_____

3.  Which areas of your life have been put on hold due to these mindsets? How does this affect your overall condition in life—and how might it impact future relationships?

_____

_____

_____

_____

_____

_____

4.  How does the neediness described in today's devotion cloud your vision? How might it draw you into a detrimental relationship?

_____

_____

_____

_____

_____

_____

5.  What goals have you set that will stand regardless of your marital status, now and in the future? Why are these goals important?

_____

_____

_____

_____

_____

_____

# MEDITATION

Many people choose a mate who can rock their world right now. God will choose a mate who can satisfy you where you're going.... Many marriages are not good because they may be good for now, but may not be good for your future. Can you grow with him? Can he go where you are going in the Spirit? Can you go where he is going in the Spirit?

That's why the Holy Ghost must lead you. Jesus is Alpha and Omega, the Beginning and the End. He's already at your end before you get there. Let His Holy Spirit lead you because He knows what is down the road. He already knows what you can and cannot take.

(*No More Sheets*, Revised Edition, Page 222)

> Are you prone to making decisions based on short-term needs? How can you bring God into the decision-making process and experience better long-term results?

_____

_____

_____

_____

_____

_____

_____

_____

_____

_____

_____

_____

_____

# Virtue's Price

*Who can find a virtuous woman? for her price is far above rubies. The heart of her husband doth safely trust in her, so that he shall have no need of spoil. She will do him good and not evil all the days of her life* (Proverbs 31:10-12).

## Today's Devotion

The virtuous woman's price is far above rubies because she pays a price to be a virtuous woman. She pays the price to be above rubies. It doesn't always mean you have to give this woman a lot of jewels. That woman knows that her spirit is more priceless than gold or diamonds. There is nothing that you can give a virtuous woman that can match what she has exercised her spirit to become. In that, she becomes what her God needs and also what a husband needs.... She's never caught off guard. She is a prepared woman.

You must prepare yourself now. A man can only expect from you what the Scriptures have promised him you should become. As you begin to practice excellence, you will strive to become what the Word says you should be.

Any man that is in the Word will be satisfied by what he sees. He will be patient to know that though you may not be perfect, he will see enough godly attributes in you to say, "If I give her a few more years, she will be all that God wants her to be."

(*No More Sheets*, Revised Edition, Pages 226-227)

# CHALLENGE THE SHEETS

1. What price have you paid to be a virtuous woman? Describe the challenges involved and the value of those challenges in becoming the woman you were created by God to be.

_____

_____

_____

_____

_____

_____

_____

_____

_____

_____

2. How is your price as a virtuous woman seen by others? How are your inward qualities displayed outwardly?

_____

_____

_____

_____

_____

_____

_____

_____

_____

_____

_____

3. In your heart, do you feel prepared for the next step in your life or do you often feel caught off-guard by new situations or relationships? Explain.

_____

_____

_____

_____

_____

_____

4. Are you relying on Scripture as the source of your wisdom and preparedness? What specific scriptural guidance are you working to make part of your everyday life?

_____

_____

_____

_____

_____

5. What godly attributes would an honest, Bible-believing man find attractive in you? Are you willing to let your imperfections show? How will this honesty form the foundation of a more viable relationship?

_____

_____

_____

_____

_____

_____

# MEDITATION

What are you bringing to the table besides eyeliner and lipstick?... Check out Proverbs 31:15: *"She riseth also while it is yet night, and giveth meat to her household, and a portion to her maidens."* Which means, she is not broke; there's money in the bank.... Let's look at what verse 16 says: *"She considereth a field, and buyeth it: with the fruit of her hands she planteth a vineyard."*

Is anything in your name besides a bunch of credit cards?... You may ask, "Why is she addressing this subject this way?" Because...if you are planning to get married and become a wife—instead of a knife—you must stop the drama right now....My little tulips, *if you want to be somebody, and if you want to go somewhere, you had better wake up and pay attention.*

(*No More Sheets*, Revised Edition, Pages 227-228)

> Do you know the *real you*—the person you bring to a potentially serious relationship? Are you ready to celebrate your godly attributes *and* face up to any areas of weakness? How will it feel to take an honest look in the mirror and move forward in virtue?

_____

_____

_____

_____

_____

_____

_____

_____

_____

# The Present Season

*To every thing there is a season, and a time to every purpose under the heaven: a time to be born, and a time to die; a time to plant, and a time to pluck up that which is planted; a time to kill, and a time to heal; a time to break down, and a time to build up; a time to weep, and a time to laugh; a time to mourn, and a time to dance; a time to cast away stones, and a time to gather stones together; a time to embrace, and a time to refrain from embracing; a time to get, and a time to lose; a time to keep, and a time to cast away; a time to rend, and a time to sew; a time to keep silence, and a time to speak; a time to love, and a time to hate; a time of war, and a time of peace* (Ecclesiastes 3:1-8).

# Today's Devotion

Your mind and your spirit must stay within the *realm of that season.* If you ignore a season, a season can kill you.... You must learn to respect the season. For example, if a person walks outside in the dead of winter wearing sandals, hot pants, and a halter top—and remains outside—that person will surely die.

This is the reason many people have not benefited from life; they do the right thing in the wrong season. Many people in Christendom...[are] looking for a blessing for which they have not sown. Galatians 6:7 says, *"Be not deceived; God is not mocked: for whatsoever a man soweth, that shall he also reap."*...

Anytime there is a force that goes against nature, you will have natural disaster—hurricanes, tornadoes, etc. The temperature from another season has dropped in a present season at the wrong time. Does that sound like you?...

You must learn to discern the season. Stop right now and ask yourself, "What season am I in?" This is your first step in correcting emotional confusion. It's as simple as this: take your emotions and set them inside the season. Instantly, they will line up and order will come. You don't have to be led away by emotional turmoil.

(*No More Sheets,* Revised Edition, Pages 229-230)

# CHALLENGE THE SHEETS

1. What season of your life are you in? (Bear in mind that, while each season has more than one identifying feature, it is marked by one unifying theme.) Is it a time of preparation or fulfillment? Healing or growth? Add your own thoughts and descriptions.

_____

_____

_____

_____

_____

_____

_____

_____

2. How well do you understand the season you are in? How have you shown respect for it? How have you missed its signs?

_____

_____

_____

_____

_____

_____

_____

_____

_____

_____

3. What are you consciously sowing in this season of your life? What "seeds" have been sown unconsciously? What harvests do you expect to reap from what you have sown?

_____

_____

_____

_____

_____

_____

4. What steps can you take to improve the quantity and quality of your harvest? What is the role and benefit of having patience while you wait?

_____

_____

_____

_____

_____

5. Are the wrong emotions showing up in your current season? What is the cause? How can you decide the state of your emotions?

_____

_____

_____

_____

_____

# MEDITATION

In your spirit man or woman, look at what you have accomplished in your character up to this point, and if it's not much in comparison to two or three years ago, then this is the time to make the decision to make steps to change your character. You don't have to be under scrutiny from another person's opinions about who you are. Like the turning of the color of leaves in the fall, you will be the first to know and see it.

(*No More Sheets*, Revised Edition, Page 230)

> Character is central to your outcomes in life. What character-building advances have you made? What goals can you set for future growth in character?

---
---
---
---
---
---
---
---
---
---
---
---
---
---
---
---
---

# Don't Give an Inch

*No discipline seems pleasant at the time, but painful. Later on, however, it produces a harvest of righteousness and peace for those who have been trained by it* (Hebrews 12:11 NIV).

## TODAY'S DEVOTION

Once you let an ungodly spirit into your life, it will attempt to take over your entire life. If you become undisciplined in washing the dishes, the next thing you know, you will become undisciplined in going to the cleaners, then undisciplined in taking a bath, then you may become undisciplined in cleaning the house, then in the way you pay your bills. Once a door opens, it eats like a cancer until it eats up all that's good in you. Pretty soon, you may not have discipline in anything. You are just a wild buck....

If you can't control your flesh—when that spirit of sloth is telling you to oversleep and be late for work, or don't pay your bills on time, or don't walk in integrity—then the same spirit will approach you with sexual sin. You have to understand that it's all a sin before God.... The difference with sexual sin is that it leaves another spirit—a tormenting spirit—in you....

Those of us who are undisciplined need to start today by saying, "There is something that I'm going to start doing now. I declare that every day at this time, this is what I am going to do." Prayer would be an excellent place to start. That is the way you break that spirit of being undisciplined.

(*No More Sheets*, Revised Edition, Pages 235-236)

# CHALLENGE THE SHEETS

1. Where are you strongest in self-discipline? In what areas is your discipline showing cracks?

_____

_____

_____

_____

_____

_____

_____

_____

2. Consider the areas of weakness you named in response to the first question. Can you pinpoint how and when you opened the door to that spirit? Explain.

_____

_____

_____

_____

_____

_____

_____

_____

3. When you decide to oversleep or leave dirty dishes in the sink, does your decision seem inconsequential? Is it? What are the aftereffects of these decisions?

_____

_____

_____

_____

_____

_____

4. How do "little things" like taking care of your house, your belongings, and your bills reflect your level of integrity? Why is integrity important?

_____

_____

_____

_____

_____

_____

5. Are you releasing the anointing within you to accomplish the things in life that must be done? Can you name a "big" problem in your life that started with a "small" indiscretion in terms of discipline?

_____

_____

_____

_____

_____

_____

# MEDITATION

When you become disciplined in all areas of your life—praying, controlling your spending habits, being on time for church—you are teaching your flesh that it can't have its way every day. You will say to your flesh, "You do it this way now *because my spirit rules. The anointing that's in me rules my flesh!*"

When you start being disciplined, then the next time you are confronted with a sexual temptation, it won't be as hard to tell your flesh, "No," because your flesh is already used to hearing that. Your flesh will say, "I know you're going to say, 'No.'" That's called discipline.

(*No More Sheets,* Revised Edition, Page 235)

> Discipline, at any given moment, seems hard. Which is harder—to bite the bullet and be disciplined in the moment or to reap the cumulative effects of an undisciplined life? What life experiences support your answer?

_____

_____

_____

_____

_____

_____

_____

_____

_____

_____

# DAY 39

## It Takes Two

*And the man said, The woman whom Thou gavest to be with me, she gave me of the tree, and I did eat. And the Lord God said unto the woman, What is this that thou hast done? And the woman said, The serpent beguiled me, and I did eat* (Genesis 3:12-13).

# Today's Devotion

There are two sides to every story. For example, if I wanted to dismantle or discredit any male, there are enough stories in the Bible to support me. If I wanted to only portray the negative side of the male gender, then I could. Since most of us spend most of our time in the negative, we want to see men as dogs.

However, I found out when I looked back over things that happened to me, there were signs about my character and my personality that said, "Y'all can take advantage of me. Just walk on me. I'm nothing but a rug anyway." There are always warnings before the relationship goes sour.

The enemy works very hard to destroy the masculinity of men.... If the enemy can destroy that—cut off the masculinity and start influencing men to walk and act feminine—it will cause us to be left feeling naked. We'll feel as if we were left without help, without assistance. Actually, in some areas, this may begin to stunt our growth as women.

(*No More Sheets,* Revised Edition, Pages 249-250)

# CHALLENGE THE SHEETS

I. Do you have a tendency to discredit the male gender as a whole? Can you pinpoint why? What does this one-sided view produce in your relationships and behavior?

_____

_____

_____

_____

_____

_____

2. Prayerfully and honestly consider the other side of the story. How might your appearance, demeanor, words, actions, and deeply-held beliefs be impacting the way members of the opposite sex treat you?

_____

_____

_____

_____

_____

_____

_____

3. What specific character traits are working to your disadvantage, relationally?

_____

_____

_____

_____

_____

_____

4. As you continue to work on character issues, how are your expectations changing in regard to how men should treat you?

_____

_____

_____

_____

_____

_____

5. Have you ever inadvertently "helped" the enemy to destroy a man's masculinity by using harsh words or by giving a man the "silent treatment"?

_____

_____

_____

_____

_____

_____

# MEDITATION

...There is something that lies deep in...the belly of a real woman that is triggered when complemented by a real man....Whether it's for relationship purposes or whether it's for marriage purposes, we cannot do without the male gender. Never give up your right as a woman to need the presence of a man. By rejecting what He made and called good, you defy God, and that offends Him.

The man you were with may have treated you badly, but that's no reason to hate all men. Reject the character of the people who have caused you great pain and harm, but don't reject the gender of the person. When you reject what God has made, that's when it gets dangerous.

(*No More Sheets*, Revised Edition, Page 250)

> Have you ever experienced the company of a real man (or woman)?
> What did that person add to your life? If you have not enjoyed this kind
> of relationship, do you believe that it is possible—and that the opposite
> sex, although imperfect, deserves your respect?

_____

_____

_____

_____

_____

_____

_____

_____

_____

_____

_____

_____

# You Define You

*Grace and peace be multiplied unto you through the knowledge of God, and of Jesus our Lord, according as His divine power hath given unto us all things that pertain unto life and godliness, through the knowledge of Him that hath called us to glory and virtue: whereby are given unto us exceeding great and precious promises: that by these ye might be partakers of the divine nature, having escaped the corruption that is in the world through lust (2 Peter 1:2-4).*

# Today's Devotion

My prayer today for every man is this [and women, this is important reading for you, too]: Don't ever allow any woman to be your definition. Only choose someone who can add definition. Now that is a very powerful statement!

When you have allowed God to impart wisdom and knowledge within you and you have spent time—I mean quality time—not dating anyone but just working on definition, then you are able to look not *at* a sister, but *within* that sister and see and hear her wisdom. From that (not by how wonderful she looks) you are able to determine whether the character inside the physical shape will fit into your life. If you choose a mate for any other reason than that, you might be getting a knife instead of a wife. The Bible says that you must be sober, meaning not intoxicated, but alert....

Some women will spend hundreds to get a man's millions. If she is more concerned about your bank book than your expectations, get rid of her as fast as you can.... Take your time in any relationship. Once you're married, you'll have the rest of your lives together. So make a wise choice.

(*No More Sheets*, Revised Edition, Pages 254-255)

# CHALLENGE THE SHEETS

1. No man or woman should allow another person to define them. If you are currently in a relationship, do you find definition in that person or do they *add* to your definition as a unique individual? Explain.

_____

_____

_____

_____

_____

_____

_____

_____

2. How well-defined are you on your own? How has God's wisdom helped you to define who you are?

_____

_____

_____

_____

_____

_____

_____

_____

_____

_____

3. There is no avoiding the fact that the first thing we see is a person's outer appearance. To what degree are your relationship decisions made on the basis of what you see? In the past, what pitfalls have resulted from not looking within the person to where character is revealed?

_____

_____

_____

_____

4. The best relationships are formed by people who complement one another—people who fit together and add to each other's definition. What kind of person would complement you well?

_____

_____

_____

_____

5. We need to take the time to understand the motives of anyone with whom we become involved. To the men: Have you ever been sucked in by a gold digger? What drew you to her? How did fulfilling her demands make you feel? To the women: Have you ever been sucked into a wrong relationship because of the man's financial ability? Did his gifts make you feel better or worse in the long run? How so?

_____

_____

_____

_____

_____

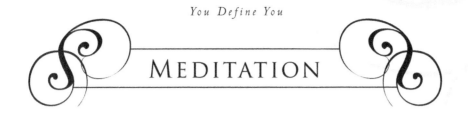

# MEDITATION

Listen, I also believe that there are some sisters that owe some brothers some apologies. Now why am I saying this? I know you do, because I did. The devil, your adversary, is seeking whom he may devour.

You see, all we have been hearing for the longest is what *he* did. But there are a large number of women whose motives from the get-go were to land a brother who had definition. Some of them spent hundreds of dollars to get your millions....

When you allow God—and I must repeat this—to purify and purge you, then your discernment will return.... Remember, marriage is for better or for worse. If you have the right spirit and your integrity and character are correct, and if you were to lose everything, your woman [or man] would still stand by you....

(*No More Sheets*, Revised Edition, Pages 255-256)

> Allow God to continue to purify and purge you. Ask yourself, "Do I have the right spirit? Are my integrity and character in order? Am I seeking a relationship for the right reasons?" Keep an open heart and God will guide you into His plan for your life!

# About Juanita Bynum

Juanita Bynum Ministries
P.O. Box 668
Lilburn, GA 30047

www.juanitabynum.com

888.652.9686